Called to Conquer

Called to Conquer

Preparing for Spiritual Victory

DOROTHY DAVIS

REGULAR BAPTIST PRESS
1300 North Meacham Road
Schaumburg, Illinois 60173-4806

Dedication

To my sister-soldier Doris.

CALLED TO CONQUER: PREPARING FOR SPIRITUAL VICTORY
© 2007
Regular Baptist Press • Schaumburg, Illinois
www.RegularBaptistPress.org • 1-800-727-4440
Printed in U.S.A.
RBP5366 • ISBN: 978-1-59402-653-9

Contents

Preface

WAR! THE word went buzzing around the city of Washington, DC on a lovely summer day in the year 1861. The citizens of the capital were filled with curiosity. What would a war be like? Dressed in their fashionable clothes and toting their picnic hampers, they excitedly climbed into their fancy carriages and ventured forth to a place called Bull Run. But before long, two fierce armies clashed with a vengeance, and soon the ground was covered with the wounded and dying. The genteel folk fled back to Washington with a new understanding: there was a real war going on and it was no picnic!

Perhaps you have never realized that every day when your feet hit the floor, you are entering a battle zone. Not only are there enemies *around* you, but there is also a conflict *within* you! The Christian life is a holy war, a *real* war, and it's no picnic! The fight is spiritual; the weapons are supernatural. As women of God, we have been called to conquer. It's time to face the battle!

How to Use This Study

Each lesson in this study is divided into five sections. Follow these suggestions as you prepare each lesson.

I. Recruit Evaluation

This section will prepare your heart to study God's Word. The answers are personal; they will not be discussed in class.

II. Basic Training

The questions in this section concentrate on the text of God's Word and will help you understand what God's Word says.

III. Deployment

As you answer the questions in this section, you will see how the truths of God's Word apply to your life.

IV. Debriefing

This section is for personal use—not group discussion. It is designed to help you put God's truth into practice in your own life.

V. Battlefield Report

These final words will help seal firmly in your mind what you have learned from the Scriptures.

Objective: Holiness

"But as he which hath called you is holy, so be ye holy in all manner of conversation; because it is written, Be ye holy; for I am holy" (1 Peter 1:15, 16).

IN ANY battle of armies, there is always an objective—some goal to be achieved or territory to be attained. The spiritual conflict we face is no different. Our enemy, Satan, has an objective, and so do we. We must understand the causes of the war we're in and why we are expected to fight it. As always, God makes all these things clear to us in His Word, the Bible.

I. Recruit Evaluation

1. In what ways are you a "holy" woman? Explain.

2. In what ways are you not holy?

II. Basic Training

In order to comprehend our enemy's aim, we must go back to the site of mankind's first spiritual conflict. After God created the heavens, the earth, and its creatures, He created a man and a woman, who were totally good and living in a perfect world (Genesis 1:31). But Satan, already at war with God, was out to change that!

1. Read Genesis 3:1–6 and answer the following questions.
    (a) Who was the serpent? (See Revelation 12:9.)

    (b) What instructions had God given Adam about eating from the tree of the knowledge of good and evil (Genesis 2:16, 17)?

    (c) What statements did Satan make to cause Eve to eat the fruit (Genesis 3:4, 5)?

2. Adam and Eve disobeyed God by doing what God had told them not to do. As soon as they disobeyed, drastic changes occurred in their relationship to God, in their perfect environment, and in themselves.
    (a) How does God describe the change in Adam and Eve in Genesis 3:22?

    (b) How is this different from 1:31?

3. According to Romans 5:12, what happened when Adam disobeyed God?

4. Read Genesis 3:7–19. List five ways in which the good and peaceful world of Adam and Eve became a place of sorrow and conflict for them.

5. What predictions and promise did God make for His enemy Satan in Genesis 3:15?

In a single moment, peace and Paradise were lost! War had begun! Disharmony would now be the norm: separation between God and mankind, personal and interpersonal stress and conflict, struggle with a sin-cursed earth. Satan had plotted a sneak attack on our first parents, and his objective had been achieved.

But had God been taken by surprise? No, consider the promise of Genesis 3:15. The Almighty One had already known that there would be sin and stress and struggle, and He already had a battle plan in place for this spiritual war.

6. When Adam and Eve disobeyed the Lord, sin entered the human race and has affected every human being born since. Look up these verses and indicate the consequences sin has had on us.

Psalm 14:2, 3

Isaiah 59:2 (see also Ezra 9:15)

James 1:15 (see also Romans 6:23)

Romans 1:18 (see also Ephesians 5:6; Colossians 3:6)

7. What is required by God in order for us to to fellowship with Him?
Romans 5:17–19 (see also Matthew 5:20)

1 Thessalonians 4:7 (see also Hebrews 12:14)

If righteousness and holiness are required to be accepted by God, and if sin prevents our ability to fellowship with Him, how then can we ever hope to have the kind of relationship that Adam and Eve had with Him before sin entered into their lives? Did Satan ruin that opportunity forever? No, God had a plan. Recall that God had said sin would require death. During Old Testament times, God mercifully allowed a person to offer the life of an animal in place of his or her own. The animal sacrificed its "life blood" and died the death the person should have died for sin. The animal became the person's substitute, and God then accepted the sinner as forgiven and "holy." Of course, animals had to be sacrificed continually to keep "covering over" the sins of the people. It wasn't a perfect solution to the sin problem.

At just the right time in human history, God sent His own Son, Jesus Christ, down to the world to live. Although He was God, Jesus Christ took on a human body and lived a sinless life. But God allowed mortal men to put His Son to death on a cross so that He could die for our sins. He became our substitute and shed His life blood to take God's judgment of our sin (Hebrews 9:11–14; 10:1–14).

8. What was God's intended purpose for His Son's death according to these verses?

Romans 5:6–10

Galatians 1:3, 4

1 Peter 2:24; 3:18

9. In Hebrews 2:10 Christ is called the Captain of our salvation (deliverance). He is the promised "seed" of the woman in Genesis 3:15! By His perfect life, atoning death, and victorious resurrection, He guaranteed Satan's ultimate defeat. How has our Captain crippled the enemy?

Hebrews 2:14, 15

1 John 3:8

Satan's objective in the Garden of Eden had been to introduce evil and sin to humankind and rob them of an eternal relationship with God, their Creator. In fact, Satan knew that the result of man's sin would be eternal separation from God in Hell, a literal place of eternal punishment prepared for Satan and his rebel army (Matthew 25:41, 46).

10. Christ's sacrificial death enables us to spend eternity with God. How can we avail ourselves of God's offer of eternal life in Heaven?
John 3:16–18

John 11:25–27

Romans 10:9–13

11. When we receive Jesus Christ as Savior, when we put our faith and trust in His death for our sins, how does God then see us?
Romans 4:5

1 Corinthians 6:9–11

2 Corinthians 5:21

At the moment a woman receives Jesus Christ into her life, some remarkable things occur in God's sight. She is no longer His enemy but His child (John 1:12). She is no more under judgment but declared "not guilty." She is reconciled to a holy God and fully acceptable to Him. In fact, God now sees her "in Christ," and as He looks upon her, He sees all the righteousness and holiness of His perfect Son (Romans 3:21–25; Ephesians 1:4–7).

"But wait," you may say. "If God sees me as being holy, then why don't I live that way? Why do I still do things that are wrong?" God has graciously granted us a "position" of holiness before Him, but in "practice" we are still very much unholy. We still have a struggle with sin in our human bodies. (We'll discuss this in lesson 5.)

So what are the causes of the war? Although he is a doomed enemy, Satan's main objective (until he's cast into Hell) is to keep people from being saved from their sin. However, if by God's grace and power a woman receives Christ, the enemy's objective then becomes to thwart her progress as a believer, to keep her unholy in practice by being disobedient to God and His Word.

12. But what is *God's* objective? He wants us to become more and more like His Son (2 Corinthians 3:18). According to 1 Peter 1:14–16, what quality does God want us to develop in our everyday living? Why does He want this?

III. Deployment

1. The presence of sin can be detected in very real ways. Explain how you see the effects of sin in each of the following areas.

Your relationship to God

Your own heart

Your relationships with others

The world

When Adam and Eve chose to sin, God could have discarded His plan for the whole human race, but He didn't. Instead, He sent His own beloved Son to live among us and suffer an agonizing death on a cross for our sins.

2. When you ponder this, what does it convey to you about God's love for you? His hatred of sin?

3. Many today deny the reality of Hell and refuse to believe that a loving God would send people to such a place. How does a proper understanding of God's holiness and justice point to the reality of Hell?

4. Having studied this lesson, what answers would you now give to the questions posed in section I?

(a) In what ways are you a "holy" woman? Explain.

(b) In what ways are you not holy?

IV. Debriefing

Consider the following questions, based on your study of this lesson.

- Have you been forgiven by God for your sins and reconciled to Him? If so, on what basis has this occurred?
- If you answered no, how will you take care of the sin problem that separates you and God?
- Do you understand the enemy's objective in your life? Can you state it?
- What is God's objective for you now that you belong to Him?

V. Battlefield Report

The war is on! Satan's objective is our disobedience to God. The Father's objective is the holiness of His children, their likeness to His righteous Son. The problem is sin, and the conflict is continual. Are *you* ready to do battle?

Equipped for the Battle

"For the weapons of our warfare are not carnal, but mighty through God to the pulling down of strong holds" (2 Corinthians 10:4).

IN RECENT years we have become familiar with the term WMD, weapons of mass destruction. Throughout the centuries, mankind has devised and amassed cunning accoutrements of war for the purpose of defense and destruction.

If our Heavenly Father expects us to fight a war, wouldn't it be reasonable to expect that He would provide us with weapons that will enable us to conquer? And so He has. Our weapons are not worldly, but spiritual. They are for our defense against evil and the defeat of sin. Are you equipped for the battle? Let's find out.

I. Recruit Evaluation

List any weapons you think you may have in your spiritual armory that will enable you to fight against the world, the flesh, and the Devil.

II. Basic Training

First of all, any soldier who is being trained for battle must develop strength. The rigors of war demand endurance and might for physical combat. So does our spiritual combat.

1. You are a woman who is being called to fight spiritual battles. Where will you get the inner strength you need for such battles?

Psalm 138:3

Psalm 144:1

Isaiah 26:4

Isaiah 40:29

This inner strength comes not from self-confidence or positive thinking. If you have trusted Jesus Christ for salvation, you have within you power for any difficulty you may face.

2. What is the Source of this power called (Acts 1:8; Ephesians 3:16)?

3. How does a person receive the Spirit according to John 7:38 and 39?

4. In what situations did the Holy Spirit equip the persons in the following texts for the difficulties they faced?

Luke 4:1, 2

Acts 4:1–14

Acts 13:6–12

Think of the firepower of man's weaponry: grenades, tanks, bombers. These are capable of removing obstacles in any war. Romans 15:13 speaks of the "power of the Holy Ghost." The Greek word for "power," *dunamis,* is the same root from which we get our word "dynamite"! The Holy Spirit dwells in us and is our source of dynamic power.

5. What are some of the spiritual obstacles the Spirit's power can remove in your life?

Romans 8:2 (see also Romans 6:22, 23; 2 Corinthians 3:17)

Romans 8:15 (see also 2 Timothy 1:7)

Romans 8:26, 27

1 Corinthians 2:9–12 (see also 1 John 2:20, 27)

1 John 4:2, 6 (see also John 16:13)

6. God has given us His Holy Spirit, but we may hinder the full release of His power in our lives.

(a) How do we do this according to Ephesians 4:30 and 1 Thessalonians 5:19?

(b) How can we be assured that we are not hindering the Holy Spirit's work in our lives?

7. So far, we have seen that we are strong in the Lord and empowered by His Spirit. But what weapons do we wield in our battle?

(a) What weapon is described in Ephesians 6:17 and Hebrews 4:12?

(b) Why is it called the Sword of the Spirit (2 Peter 1:20, 21)?

A sword is both an offensive and defensive weapon. We may use it to attack an enemy or to defend ourselves from attack.

8. Read Matthew 4:1–11 and explain how the Lord Jesus used the Scriptures as both His offensive and defensive weapon against Satan.

9. Another weapon in our arsenal is prayer. Read each passage below, and state what we could regularly pray as a defense against the Devil.

Luke 22:31, 32

Luke 22:39–46

John 17:15 (see also Matthew 6:13)

10. Paul instructed us how to use this weapon in Ephesians 6:18. Jot down your thoughts about each of the key words or phrases from the verse.

Always

With all prayer

Supplication

In the Spirit

Watching thereunto

With all perseverance

For all saints

11. What encouragement do we have in these verses to use our weapon of prayer?

     Hebrews 4:15, 16

     James 5:16–18

In days of old it was called armor; today it's called protective gear. Whatever the name, a soldier needs a covering to protect his vital organs. This is true in the spiritual life as well. A well-equipped warrior protects body, soul, and spirit.

12. Read Ephesians 6:11 and 13 and answer the following questions about your armor.

     (a) What is the armor called?

     (b) What will it aid you in doing?

13. Of what is the armor constructed?

     Romans 13:12

     2 Corinthians 6:7

     Ephesians 6:14, 15

1 Thessalonians 5:8

14. A few additional items complete a soldier's equipment. What are they?

Ephesians 6:16

Ephesians 6:17 (see also 1 Thessalonians 5:8)

There is one additional item a soldier bears: a dog tag, his identification. If captured by the enemy, a soldier has been trained to answer every interrogation by stating his name, rank, and serial number—his identity—nothing more. As long as he persistently presents these credentials only, the enemy can gain no hold over him.

As believers, we have been given a new identity (2 Corinthians 5:17). We are now "in Christ." In fact, we bear His name. (The word "Christian" means "Christ follower.") In God's reckoning we are one with Christ in His death, burial, resurrection, and ascension (Romans 6:4, 5; Ephesians 2:4–6). As long as we value and depend upon our identification with Christ, the enemy can gain no hold over us.

15. What facts are stated about us when we are "in Christ"?

1 Corinthians 15:57

2 Corinthians 2:14

III. Deployment

1. A soldier would never enter a battle zone without his or her weapon. That would be ludicrous! Yet sadly, some believers are so neglectful of God's Word that they are virtually weaponless in their spiritual conflicts. What causes believers to neglect God's Word?

2. Not only does a warrior need a weapon, but he or she must be trained to know its parts and use. Recall from our Scripture study how effectively Christ used the Word to "remind" Himself of the Father's will and to refute Satan's tempting arguments. What must you do to learn the "parts" of your weapon and become proficient at using it (2 Timothy 2:15; 3:16)?

3. The powerful weapon of prayer is missing in the arsenal of some believers today. Again, as with Bible study, personal prayer time is neglected, sometimes for days or weeks at a time. It's not surprising, then, that the Lord's army, the church, is made up of weak warriors. If we neglect Spirit-filled prayer, what kind of results will we see in the following areas?

Our personal lives

Our families

Our churches

Our country

4. As you consider the armor God wants you to wear, note beside each quality how that particular virtue will enable you to stand your ground against sin and Satan's attacks.

Light

Righteousness

Truth

Peace

Faith

Love

5. How do you "put on" this armor daily?

6. Do you think God has provided adequate resources for our war? Why or why not?

IV. Debriefing

Consider the following questions, based on your study of this lesson.

- Do you understand how essential the ministry of the Holy Spirit is in your life? Are you allowing Him to fill you?
- Are you learning about your weapon, the Word of God? In what way do you think you need to learn it more?
- Are you practicing the power of prayer? Are you praying spiritual requests for yourself and others?
- Are you putting on your armor daily?
- Do you understand that your identification is now "in Christ" and that Satan no longer has a right to hold you captive?

V. Battlefield Report

In the spiritual battles of life, God has given you all you need to triumph. But have you been neglecting your preparation? Are you being strengthened by His Spirit, skillfully wielding your Sword of the Word, and resisting the enemy by prayer? Are you being protected by your armor, your helmet, and your shield? We have been told to "be strong in the Lord, and in the power of his might" (Ephesians 6:10). Don't get caught off guard; be equipped for the battle!

The Strategic Battlefield

"And be renewed in the spirit of your mind; And that ye put on the new man, which after God is created in righteousness and true holiness" (Ephesians 4:23, 24).

IN THE wars of America's past, famous battles have occurred at critical locations. Saratoga, Gettysburg, Normandy—victory or defeat at these critical sites had a substantial effect on the course of each war and its eventual outcome.

As we have seen, God's objective is our righteousness and holiness. But you and I are continually engaged in conflict with our opponents: the world, the flesh, and the forces of Satan. This is not mere metaphorical babble; it is reality. We face both outright assault as well as subtle pressure to yield.

In this ongoing war, your mind is the strategic battlefield. The thoughts you think will lead you either to spiritual victory or defeat. How you think is having a substantial effect, not only on your present spiritual condition, but ultimately, on the course of your life. In this invisible war, the mind truly matters!

I. Recruit Evaluation

Which of these emotions or reactions are regularly problematic for you?
- A critical spirit/anger/resentment
- Anxiety/worry/fear
- Self-condemnation/guilt
- Discouragement/self-pity/depression

- Envy/jealousy
- Complaining/discontentment/covetousness
- Self-centeredness/ambition/desire to control

II. Basic Training

The Word of God has much to say about our minds. When we become new creations in Christ (2 Corinthians 5:17), God wants us to begin thinking in a new way. As we study the following verses, the Lord will instruct us how to take a key step toward spiritual victory *by thinking Biblically!*

1. Read Ephesians 4:17–24 and answer these questions.
    (a) What command is given to us (v. 17)?

    (b) What are the results of an unbeliever's thinking habits (vv. 18, 19)?

    (c) Paul begins verse 20 with a contrast word, "but." Christians' attitudes and actions are to be distinctly different than unbelievers'. How are we to become different (v. 23)?

    (d) What will be the result of being renewed in our minds (v. 24)?

2. Now read Romans 12:2.
    (a) What are we instructed to do?

(b) How will we be transformed?

(c) What will be the result of a renewed mind?

Why is it so important to have a renewed mind? Prior to salvation, you had a "carnal mind" that had no inclination to please God (Romans 8:7). But now, as a believer, you have a new nature that is both willing and able to love and obey God (Romans 7:22, 23). Your "mind/heart" organ is the control center of your being. In fact, your mind directs your will. And since God has granted you a free will to choose to obey or disobey Him, your mind needs to be filled with thoughts of how to love and please God.

3. Read the following verses and explain why the "mind/heart" is so critical.

Proverbs 4:23

Proverbs 23:7

Matthew 12:33–35

You must fully grasp the fact that your thoughts and continual thought patterns are determining your character and choices. What goes on in your mind is influencing your will, your words, your attitudes, and your actions. And it affects what you do with your emotions. This is why your mind is a strategic battlefield where spiritual victory or defeat occurs.

4. Mind renewal involves breaking "old life" thought patterns and changing the way we think. What are some of these "thinking habits" that hang on from our old life?

     1 Corinthians 3:3 (see also Romans 8:7; James 4:1–4)

     1 Corinthians 3:19, 20 (see also Psalm 2:1; Romans 1:21; 2 Corinthians 10:5)

     2 Timothy 1:7 (Mark 4:40; 1 John 4:18)

5. We are instructed by God's Word that we are in control of and responsible for our thinking. How do these verses direct us to control our thoughts?

     2 Corinthians 10:5

     Philippians 4:8

     Colossians 3:2

     1 Peter 1:13

It was mentioned earlier that a key step toward spiritually victorious living is *thinking Biblically*. As a believer, you must fill your heart and mind with Word-saturated thoughts.

6. What instruction did God give to His people concerning His Word? Deuteronomy 11:18

    Joshua 1:8

    Psalm 119:11

    Colossians 3:16

As the Word infiltrates our thinking and our minds are renewed, old thought patterns will begin to break down. As we think according to His Word, attitudes, actions, and speech will also begin to change. Our decisions will be determined by God's directives, and our choices will be made according to God's commands.

Furthermore, we will find ourselves *responding* to life rather than *reacting* to it (Psalm 119:59, 133). So often we find that our emotions, rather than Biblical thoughts, control us. When personalities, problems, and perplexities test us, we are quick to react with pride, anger, fear, guilt, discouragement, or worry. Then we fuel these emotions by fleshly thinking.

As believers, our responsibility is to rein in our harmful emotions by thinking Biblical thoughts. Eventually, our emotions will subside, and we will be able to deal with life from God's perspective. (Read Psalm 73 for an example of this process in action.)

7. What emotion is addressed in each of these verses, and what
Biblical thoughts will lead you to properly handle it?

Psalm 56:3, 4

Romans 8:33, 34

Ephesians 4:31, 32

1 Peter 5:5, 6

Rampant emotions, fleshly thinking, ungodly attitudes. It is a cycle
that can lead a believer to a life of turmoil and spiritual failure. But God,
by His Word and His Spirit, can free us from this defeating cycle and cause
us to be women who experience spiritual victory in the battles of life.

So then, is this simply a "positive thinking" philosophy? No. We cannot
bring about real, permanent change of character merely by positive thinking. First of all, we are to think Biblically, not positively. We are not filling
our minds with good thoughts about ourselves but thoughts about God
and His will. Second, the Word itself is a Book of inherent *power* because it
has proceeded from God (1 Thessalonians 2:13; Hebrews 4:12). The words
are words that can change us.

8. What personal benefits did the psalmist gain as he filled his life
with Scripture?

Psalm 119:6

Psalm 119:28

Psalm 119:45

Psalm 119:49

Psalm 119:98

Psalm 119:165

In addition to the power of the Word dwelling richly in us, we have the power of the Spirit living within us. Working together, these two powerful agents accomplish something truly amazing in us: a changed life! This is the glorious advantage Christians have over unbelievers.

9. What do these verses teach you about God's power and its result in your life?
2 Corinthians 3:17, 18

Ephesians 1:19, 20

Ephesians 3:20

Philippians 2:13

Recall that Romans 12:2 states, "Be ye transformed by the renewing of your mind." We are not commanded to transform ourselves but to permit the transformation to take place as our minds are renewed by the Word. Our job is to absorb God's Word and yield to the Spirit's leading (Galatians 5:16). Indeed, the Spirit desires to lead us in our thinking and in the meditations of our hearts.

The more we submit ourselves to His influence through the Word and prayer, the more we will begin to think, speak, and act as Christ did. Our fleshly thoughts and reactions will be replaced by His God-pleasing mind-set and His godly responses (1 Corinthians 2:16; Philippians 2:5). As the Word fills our minds and the Lord possesses our hearts, we will walk in the righteousness and holiness God desires.

III. Deployment

1. Who's controlling your mind? In our present culture, ideas come at us in a constant barrage. Though we may not be aware of it, we are being pressured to conform to this world. Can you think of a motto, advertising slogan, or song that might plant unbiblical thinking in people's minds?

2. Carnal thinking, vain imaginations, a spirit of fear—as believers, we must put off the mind-set of the old life. What will you do to break down these ungodly thought patterns?

3. Perhaps you're wondering, "Is it possible to think Biblical thoughts throughout a busy day of duties and distractions?" Of course our minds will be occupied with many things throughout a day. But we can take steps that will help us be Scripturally minded. List some ways of directing your thoughts toward the Lord and His Word.

4. Imagine this scenario. A position opens at your place of employment, and you really want to get it. You feel you are very well qualified, and you've prayed about it too. You and several others are interviewed. Finally, a coworker, whom you feel is not as well qualified, lands the position. You're crushed and angry! You determine that from now on, she'll get the cold shoulder from you! As you lie in bed that night, you could continue to stew about how unfair it is. Or, if you *choose* to think Biblically, what will you think about?

5. What kind of personal prayer requests can you add to your prayer list that deal with this area of Biblical thinking?

6. Refer to section I again. What problematic emotions persistently surface for you? How can you begin to rein in these emotions by Biblical thinking? (Note: Your leader will not discuss this question.)

IV. Debriefing

Consider the following questions, based on your study of this lesson.

- When you think of your life before and after salvation, would you say that you have changed or have basically remained the same?
- Are you taking in Scripture on a consistent basis?
- Would you say that, in general, you are working to bring your thought-life into obedience to Christ?
- Do you more often emotionally react or calmly respond?
- Do you endeavor to think Biblically in times of frustration, fear, or friction?
- Do you understand that the Word and the indwelling Spirit are God's powerful provisions to transform you? Do you earnestly desire to be changed?

V. Battlefield Report

The field of battle is your mind. Attacks will come—suddenly and sometimes forcefully. They may come from the weapons of the world, the bombardments of the flesh, or the subtle ambushes of our adversary, Satan. How successful have you been in resisting the assault? Do you find that your defense fails rather quickly?

Your first strong line of defense is Biblical thinking. It can subdue destructive emotions. It can detect the Devil's deceitful devices. It can take into captivity the thoughts that lead to defeat. As you become entrenched in Scripture and empowered by the Spirit, attacks will be rebuffed. The enemy will gain no foothold, and victory can be secured. Yes, your mind can be the scene of many victorious conquests!

Our War with the World

"No man that warreth entangleth himself with the affairs
of this life; that he may please him who hath chosen him to
be a soldier" (2 Timothy 2:4).

IN 1967 Israel fought a six-day war. In the fourteenth and fifteenth centuries, England was embroiled in a one-hundred-year war. A war may end quickly or drag on interminably. As believers, our war with the world is an ongoing one. Since we live *in the world,* we must continually do battle *with the world.* Yes, we are surrounded by the enemy, but we must not surrender! The Lord has given us orders to stay focused and resist the onslaught, and we must obey. The world has readied its weapons; do you have yours?

I. Recruit Evaluation

Which of the following exert a strong influence upon your life?
- Ambition: the drive to attain success, admiration, power, or glory
- Beauty: the fixation with physical appearance
- Cares: preoccupation with life's demands and responsibilities
- Pleasure: the gratification of wants and wishes; the need to experience fun and excitement
- Wisdom: the pursuit of man's knowledge; learning for self-advancement

II. Basic Training

If we are to fight an enemy, we must identify who it is and where it is found. Who is this enemy the Bible calls "the world"? The original Greek words encompass the idea of this present age with its cares, temptations, and desires. Or, the word may refer to the fallen universal order that is hostile to God. In other words, the world is that sphere of life, both material and immaterial, that seeks to alienate us from God (1 John 5:19). This enemy surrounds us and continually bombards us with its ideas, allurements, distractions, and provocations.

   1. Why are we to consider the world as a spiritual enemy?
      John 15:18, 19

      James 4:4

      1 John 3:1

How does this enemy operate? It employs a multifaceted attack to achieve its objectives and utilizes a vast array of highly effective weapons to bring about its results. The ultimate aim of this enemy is to get us to lose our spiritual focus and forsake God.

   2. The world has three arsenals that hold its weapons. According to 1 John 2:16, from what three sources will the world pull its weapons?

Now let's examine this enemy's four objectives. These objectives are meant to divert a believer's spiritual focus from God and His Word so that she can eventually be taken captive.

Enemy objective #1: To mold the believer's mind-set. We have already discussed that God's goal is to conform us to the likeness of His Son. Contrary to this goal, the world seeks to shape us into its secular, humanistic mind-set by exerting its earthly perspectives and pressures upon us.

Unbelievers are like putty, pliable under the world's pressures to mold them to its will. But as women of God, we are no longer to be shaped by the world's influences (Romans 12:2; 1 Peter 1:14). Yet many times this enemy uses weapons from its arsenal of the pride of life to drive us into its worldly way of thinking.

3. As believers, what ungodly motivations must we avoid?
   Genesis 3:5

   2 Kings 17:15

   1 Corinthians 1:20

   1 Timothy 6:9

   1 Peter 3:3

Yes, we often get caught up in seeking the world's esteem through power, popularity, acceptance, appearance, wisdom, and wealth. We crave its recognition, its glory, and its honor.

4. What must we remember about human glory according to 1 Peter 1:24?

5. What does the Bible tell us about obtaining true honor?
    Proverbs 22:4

    John 12:26 (see also John 5:44)

Enemy objective #2: To lure our hearts' affections away from Christ. From the arsenals of the lust of the flesh and the lust of the eyes, our enemy unveils more powerful weapons to achieve this second objective: pleasures, riches, money, and material objects. Believers, beware!

6. Read Ecclesiastes 2:1–11. To what conclusion did Solomon come regarding the pursuit of self-gratification through pleasure?

7. What reminders does the Bible give concerning wealth?
    Proverbs 23:5

    Matthew 6:19, 20

    1 Timothy 6:7

8. What will be the spiritual result in our lives if we become ensnared by a desire for worldly accumulation?
    Matthew 6:24

1 Timothy 6:9

1 John 2:15

Enemy objective #3: To distract believers so that they become spiritually sidetracked and stagnant.

9. Read Matthew 13:22. What strategy accomplishes this objective?

10. What are some of the cares of this life that may distract us from giving our time and attention to God?
Matthew 6:31–34

Luke 10:38–42

Enemy objective #4: To dishearten believers so that they fall away (backslide) from the faith. If the world can't bend us, buy us, or bother us, it might try to break us.

11. Read Mark 4:16 and 17. Explain how the world tries to break us.

12. What did the Lord Jesus instruct His followers about the world's efforts to derail our faith? Summarize John 15:18–20 and 16:33.

13. How does Christ expect us to respond to the persecution of the world? Read Luke 6:22–35 and write what your thoughts/attitudes, words, and actions should be.

Thoughts/attitudes

Words

Actions

14. As a summary of what you've studied, read Hebrews 11:24–27 and answer the following questions.

(a) How did Moses resist man's glory and honor (v. 24)?

(b) What was his attitude toward pleasures (v. 25)?

(c) What did he choose over worldly riches (vv. 25, 26)?

(d) How did he handle persecution (v. 27)?

(e) What was his focus as he was bombarded by all of these worldly weapons (v. 27)?

(f) What do you learn from Moses' response to the world's temptation?

15. Read 2 Timothy 2:1–4.
    (a) What is a good soldier expected to do (v. 3)?

    (b) What must a good soldier avoid in order to please the Commander (v. 4)?

    (c) How can a Christian be strong "in grace"? (See Hebrews 4:16.)

III. Deployment

We have seen the weapons that assault us in this ongoing war: the ambitions and drives for glory and recognition, the riches and pleasures of prosperity, the cares of life, and the afflictions of an antagonistic world system. The aim is to mold us, lure us, distract us, and dishearten us. Surely we could be overcome by the sheer magnitude of this bombardment!

But God has exhorted us to be strong in His grace, and He has enabled us with His Word to fend off attacks. For every worldly temptation that targets us, the Bible provides a mental focus to counter the attack. When we stay spiritually focused, we will not become entangled in the distractions of this life.

1. The chart below presents the world's weapons. In the middle column, jot down a Biblical thought that will be your defense against the temptation. In the last column, give a verse you can recall that supports your answer. Two examples are provided for you.

Weapon	Mental Focus	Verses
(a) Desire for beauty	Outward beauty fades; focus on inner beauty.	Proverbs 31:30
(b) Search for acceptance	Focus on being accepted by God.	Ephesians 1:6
(c) Self-exaltation; ambition		
(d) Riches; wealth		
(e) Worldly wisdom		
(f) Things		
(g) Pleasure		
(h) Cares		
(i) Persecution; ridicule		

2. In what ways do Christians seek to imitate the world?

3. Give a real-life example that demonstrates how human glory fades quickly.

4. By claiming that we don't live for man's honor, are we saying we don't have to be concerned about what others think of us? Explain.

5. How can you be sure that the distractions of life don't pull you away from your relationship with God?

6. How do you graciously deal with the antagonism of unbelievers toward your faith in Christ?

IV. Debriefing

Consider the following questions, based on your study of this lesson.

- Is the world pressing you into its mold by pressures of achievement, admiration, acceptance, or accumulation?
- Is it luring you away from Christ through its pleasures, treasures, and wealth?
- Is it distracting you and spiritually disabling you by its cares and demands?
- Is it disheartening you by its antagonism to your faith?

V. Battlefield Report

Day after day, we are battered by the world's weapons. But we have grace to stand with our Sword in hand. By exercising a disciplined mind that stays focused on Biblical thoughts, we can overcome the onslaught of this assault. As a good soldier of Jesus Christ, refuse to become entangled with the affairs of this life. Yes, it is a long war. But as we stand fast in the Lord's overcoming power, we will surely win!

Our Fight against the Flesh

"For the flesh lusteth against the Spirit, and the Spirit against the flesh: and these are contrary the one to the other: so that ye cannot do the things that ye would" (Galatians 5:17).

YOU MIGHT have heard someone say, "I'm my own worst enemy!" From a spiritual viewpoint, we could all probably make that claim. Though we must battle both the world and the Devil, the toughest opponent we must face may very well be our own flesh.

What is "the flesh" and why does it cause us such trouble? You probably already know the answer from experience. The Bible sets forth in very clear terms why our fight against the flesh is a bitter one.

I. Recruit Evaluation

Decide whether the following statements are true or false.

- All people are somewhat good and somewhat bad in God's eyes.
- The "works of the flesh" are always wicked and vile.
- Only unbelievers do works of the flesh.
- There's nothing a believer can do but give in to sin.
- To overcome sin, a believer must try harder to do right.

II. Basic Training

If Adam and Eve had not sinned, we would be perfect human beings, rightly responding to God in all our ways and pleasing Him in all our actions. But our first parents disobeyed Him and introduced sin to the human race. Now we all struggle with "sin in the flesh."

What is "the flesh"? The basic meaning of the Greek word *sarx* is "the body of an animal or a human." But the apostle Paul used this Greek word to describe the human state or condition under the influence of sin.

1. How is the flesh described by Paul in Romans 7:18?

2. According to these verses, why is the flesh an enemy, that is, an opponent to our relationship with God?

Romans 7:22, 23

Romans 8:7 ("carnal" means "fleshly")

Galatians 5:17

1 Peter 2:11

Whenever people think, speak, or act apart from God and His will, they are "in the flesh."

3. Read John 6:63. What did Christ say about the flesh?

4. What is true of a person "in the flesh" according to Romans 8:8?

5. The flesh often manifests itself through human lusts or desires. How do human lusts drive a person toward destruction?
     Galatians 6:7, 8

    James 1:14, 15

The *works of the flesh* are human endeavors and activities that do not proceed from or give regard to God.

6. Describe some of the works of the flesh from these passages.
    Romans 13:13

    Galatians 5:19–21

    Ephesians 5:3–5

The works of the flesh seem quite vile, don't they? Surprisingly, the works of the flesh can also seem quite righteous!

7. What seemingly righteous works of the flesh were condemned by
the Lord Jesus?

Matthew 6:1, 2

Matthew 6:5–7

Matthew 7:21, 22

To summarize, then, the works of the flesh span a spectrum from re-
voltingly wicked to self-righteously religious. But are unbelievers the only
ones who manifest their flesh? As you probably already suspect, believers
may also display the flesh through their lives. A *carnal* Christian is one
who yields to the sinful flesh and not to the Spirit. The early church leaders
had to rebuke some believers and churches for carnal behavior.

8. What kinds of problems did carnal Christians create?
1 Corinthians 3:1–3

1 Corinthians 6:1–8

1 Corinthians 11:17–22

James 4:1–3

How sad and shameful when Christians fight each other rather than the real enemy—the sinful flesh! How Satan must delight to see believers battering each other and to see churches disintegrating into ineffectiveness!

What causes believers to live in the flesh rather than in the Spirit? Chapters 6 and 7 of Paul's epistle to the Romans pinpoint two reasons why believers remain carnal.

Romans 6 teaches that we have been judicially "set free" from sin. Having received Christ as Savior, we are no longer identified as being "in Adam" but "in Christ," sharing in His victory over sin and death (vv. 3, 4).

9. What do these verses in Romans 6 tell you about your relationship to sin?
   Verses 2, 11

   Verses 7, 18, 22

   Verse 14

10. What are you not to do (Romans 6)?
    Verse 6

    Verse 12

    Verse 13

You no longer have to be dominated by the sin in your flesh; *sin no longer has a right to rule over you!* But because God has granted you freedom of choice, you can at any moment let sin rule you once more. This is the first reason believers remain in the flesh—by deliberate choice. They submit themselves to the lusts within and remain enslaved to sin.

Romans 7 explains the second reason believers are carnal—they try to overcome sin's power in their own strength. They grit their teeth and try to do better. But Paul says we will fail (v. 19).

11. Who alone can empower us and deliver us from our sinful flesh (Romans 7:24, 25)?

How can you have victory over the sinful power of your own flesh? First, you must *genuinely desire* to obey God in all things. As long as we want *our* way, we will continue to exhibit the works of the flesh.

12. What words in Romans 6:13 show that we must desire and choose to obey God?

Second, remember that sin has no right to rule over you (Romans 6:14); *reckon that you are dead* to its power (v. 11).

Third, Colossians 3:5 instructs you to *mortify your members,* that is, subdue the parts of your body. By avoiding sources of temptation whenever and wherever you possibly can, you encourage yourself to remain dead to sin!

13. What instructions are given in these verses?
1 Timothy 6:9–11

2 Timothy 2:22

1 Peter 2:11

Fourth and finally, you must *rely by faith* upon Christ and the Spirit to empower you to overcome sin. Don't fight flesh with flesh!

14. Read Galatians 5:16–26. The Galatian believers, like the Corinthian believers, seemed to be struggling with the flesh. What did Paul teach?
   (a) What would enable them to overcome the flesh (v. 16)?

   (b) What is another way of saying this (v. 18)?

   (c) What attitudes and actions will be displayed by those who walk in the Spirit (vv. 22, 23)?

   (d) As believers walk in the Spirit, what will be the state of the flesh (v. 24)?

We discover in Romans 7 that even the godly apostle Paul struggled with his sinful flesh. In verse 24 he lamentingly asked, "O wretched man that I am! who shall deliver me from the body of this death?" His answer pointed, not to what, but *to Whom* we must look for victory: the Lord Jesus Christ (v. 25).

15. Read Romans 13:14. What will ensure that we will not carry out the lusts of the flesh? Explain what you think this means.

It is Christ's cross work and His resurrection power that we must depend upon for victory. It is a victory by faith. As we abide in Him and walk in the Spirit, sin will surely be defeated in our lives!

III. Deployment

1. Titus 3:5 states, "Not by works of righteousness which we have done, but according to his mercy he saved us." Now that you've studied the flesh, explain why a person cannot be saved from Hell by doing works of righteousness.

2. How might true believers serve God in the flesh in their churches?

3. What kinds of carnal sins are condemned in the church today? What carnal sins are more "acceptable" to us?

4. It would seem that any Christian would want to be free from sin! Why do we yield ourselves to sin's control when we don't have to?

5. What are some of the persons, places, and things believers should avoid to subdue (mortify, not stir up) the lusts and drives of the flesh?

6. How will you "put on" the Lord Jesus Christ today?

IV. Debriefing

Consider the following questions, based on your study of this lesson.

- Would you describe yourself as driven by your lusts and desires and helpless to do otherwise?
- Do you understand why you are defeated by a particular sin on a regular basis even though you determine and try not to do it anymore?
- Do you genuinely want God to have His way over your way in your life?
- Do you do "works of righteousness" to appear spiritual before others?
- Are you creating friction in your church by wanting your own way?
- Are you avoiding sources of temptation that seem to lure you into sin?
- Do you "put on" the Lord Jesus Christ each day and seek to walk in the Spirit?

V. Battlefield Report

The fight against the flesh is a progressive one; patience is needed. It is not a one-time experience in which sin is eliminated by some ZAP and we become holy. No, this fight is a campaign in which we are continually engaging the enemy, yet all the time *learning* how to walk in the victory we have through Christ.

Recognize the enemy within (sin) and remember it has no right to rule over you. Don't put yourself in tempting situations that stir up the lusts of the flesh. Keep putting on daily the Lord Jesus Christ in heart and mind. As you advance in the mighty power of His Spirit, sin will retreat more and more. He will surely give the victory!

Unseen Enemies

"For we wrestle not against flesh and blood, but against principalities, against powers, against the rulers of the darkness of this world, against spiritual wickedness in high places" (Ephesians 6:12).

BEFORE we consider our strategy against Satan, let's take a look at what the Bible reveals about two unseen armies: the forces of evil and darkness and the forces of goodness and light. Much has been written in our day about the Devil and his demons, some of which has led to mistaken notions and obsessive fear. Who exactly is this enemy and his army? What can they do to God's people? Knowing the facts of the Word should eliminate the fantasy and alleviate the unfounded fears regarding these invisible foes.

I. Recruit Evaluation

What do you know about angels and demons? Underline the correct answer to each question.

1. Angels are
   (a) spirits of people who have died;
   (b) spirit beings created by God.

2. Demons are
   (a) evil ghosts of people who have died;
   (b) fallen angels who rebelled against God.

3. Satan

    (a) is like God, except evil;

    (b) is a fallen angel, limited in knowledge.

4. Satan

    (a) has unrestrained power over the world and its people;

    (b) can only do what God allows.

5. Satan

    (a) will be defeated when Christ returns;

    (b) is already judged and defeated.

II. Basic Training

Though you can't see them, two armies are engaged in battle in this universe. The legions of righteousness and light are called angels; the forces of rebellion and darkness are called demons. The spiritual conflict in which they are continually involved is very real and very intense. And we are not mere bystanders in this battle. Some of their activities are directed toward us as well as toward each other.

Where did these armies come from? The Bible speaks of a sphere of life that exists in unseen, heavenly realms. The beings that inhabit this realm have extraordinary power and varying degrees of influence.

1. Look up the following verses: Ephesians 1:20, 21; 3:9, 10; 6:12; Colossians 2:10, 15.

    (a) What terms does the apostle Paul use to describe this realm of beings?

    (b) In Romans 8:38 what beings are mentioned along with these powers?

2. According to Colossians 1:16, how do we know that the heavenly beings were created by God?

3. Who are angels? What are they like? Look up the following verses and record your findings.
   Psalm 103:20, 21

   Luke 20:34–36

   Hebrews 1:13, 14 (see also Psalm 91:11)

When Paul referred to "principalities and powers," he usually had demons in mind, not good angels. Who are demons? Actually, they too are angels, evil angels. Scripture describes them as invisible (usually) and possessing superhuman strength and knowledge.

4. According to the Word, why did these spirit beings become wicked?
   2 Peter 2:4

   Jude 6

The goal of demons, like their leader Satan, is to damage or destroy the work of God. This includes afflicting and harassing the human beings He has created.

5. What are some of the wicked works demons may do?
   Matthew 12:22

   Matthew 17:14–18

   Acts 16:16 (see also Acts 13:7–10; 1 Samuel 28:6, 7)

   1 Corinthians 10:20

   1 Timothy 4:1

   Revelation 16:14

6. What phrases from the following verses show that a believer
cannot be demon possessed?
   1 Corinthians 6:19

   1 John 4:4

   1 John 5:18

Both the angelic and demonic armies are organized according to power and rank. The angel Michael, for example, is called an archangel (meaning first or highest angel; Jude 9). Lucifer, or Satan, was a high-ranking angel in God's host (or army). He is now prince of the demonic horde.

7. What caused Satan to fall?
   1 John 3:8

   1 Timothy 3:6

8. What titles and descriptions of Satan are given in Scripture?
   Matthew 13:19

   John 8:44

   John 12:31

   2 Corinthians 4:4

   Ephesians 2:2

   1 Thessalonians 3:5

1 Peter 5:8

Revelation 12:9, 10

9. Hordes of demons. Legions of angels. An unseen conflict is taking place on earth and in the air. Is this *really* true? Read the account in 2 Kings 6:15–17. What did the Lord allow Elisha's servant to see?

10. Read Daniel 10:1–14 and answer the following questions.
   (a) Who was sent to speak to Daniel (v. 11)?

   (b) Why was he delayed (v. 13)?

   (c) How long had he been delayed (v. 13)?

   (d) How long had Daniel been praying and seeking God's answer (vv. 2, 3)?

   (e) Who came to the messenger's aid (v. 13)?

Yes, war is going on between two unseen armies in invisible realms. (Read Revelation 12:7–9 for another example.) Satan is called "the prince of this world" (John 12:31). His demons exert influence over the kingdoms of men; his host seeks to hinder the work of God upon earth. But how much damage can they do? Must we live in constant fear that they will kill us, sabotage us, or spiritually attack us?

Satan is a created being; he is not God. He is not omnipresent, omniscient, or omnipotent. Yes, his power is great and his army is vast in number. But still, there are limits to the force of this foe.

11. Read Job 1:6–12 and 2:1–6.
(a) Where was Satan permitted to go (1:6, 7)?

(b) What was he permitted to do (1:12)?

(c) What could he *not* do (2:6)?

(d) Who set the limitations upon where Satan could go or what he could do?

12. Why does God allow Satan to harass us? This is difficult to answer completely. God may allow the Devil and demons to bring suffering upon us for His sovereign purposes (2 Corinthians 12:7). But think about Job's affliction; it was not only permitted but initiated by God! (Scan Job 42, if needed.)
(a) What did Job's trial accomplish in his life?

(b) How did it result in God's glory?

(c) How was it a rebuke to Satan's false accusations (Job 1:10, 11; 2:9, 10)?

13. Read 1 Kings 22:19–23, which describes a vision that the Lord gave to His prophet Micaiah.

(a) Who came before the Lord's throne (v. 19)?

(b) Do you think the angel mentioned in verses 21 and 22 is good or evil? Why?

(c) What did God allow the spirit to do? Why?

14. Satan is called "the prince of the power of the air" (Ephesians 2:2). How is Jesus Christ described in these verses?

Daniel 7:13, 14

Matthew 25:31–34

Revelation 19:16

15. Christ is King of the universe. Satan is but a prince and a defeated prince at that. On what basis has Satan already been judged and defeated? John 12:27–33 (see also Colossians 2:14, 15)

Hebrews 2:14

16. What future doom awaits the wicked one and his army?
Revelation 12:7, 9

Revelation 20:1–3

Revelation 20:7–12

III. Deployment

1. What are some of the mistaken notions people have about angels?

2. What might be the ministry of angels in your life? in the world?

3. Some people and churches obsess over demonic activity and attack. In light of what you've learned, why should you, as a believer, not be paralyzed by fear of these evil forces? (See, for example, Romans 8:38, 39; Ephesians 6:13; 1 Peter 3:22; 1 John 2:14 and 4:4.)

4. How should you view Satan and his forces?

IV. Debriefing

Consider the following questions, based on your study of this lesson.

- Do you believe there is an unseen battle raging both on earth and in heavenly realms?
- Do you better understand the Bible's teaching on angels, demons, and the spiritual conflict that surrounds us?
- Do you understand that, although powerful, Satan and demons are limited by God's sovereign will in what they can do to you as a believer in Christ?
- Are you resting and rejoicing in the love and power of your sovereign Lord and His watchful care over you?

V. Battlefield Report

If you pick up the newspaper, you may read with concern the latest developments of Earth's many wars. Yet in Ephesians 6:12 Paul reminded believers that the most crucial battles taking place are not human conflicts but cosmic conflicts fought in heavenly places. The battle of good versus evil is not symbolic but very real. One has only to observe the spiritual darkness gripping this world to grasp the effectiveness of this assault. Satan means business, and his army is active.

But as believers, we don't have to quake in terror of these attacks. The Lord of Hosts has mobilized His celestial army of light, numbering ten thousand times ten thousand angels. These mighty ones fight for us, protect us, and do His bidding. We must not be afraid, but aware—as we'll see in our next lesson. The *ultimate* outcome is already assured!

Defenses against the Devil

"Put on the whole armour of God, that ye may be able to stand against the wiles of the devil" (Ephesians 6:11).

WE HAVE seen what a formidable foe we face in Satan and his horde. Until Christ returns to earth to set up His Kingdom, the forces of evil will continue to roam this earth, seeking to inflict damage upon God's works. How can we stand against the evil about us? A wise woman will always be on the alert for the enemy's attack. Are you?

I. Recruit Evaluation

Underline each of the phrases below that you think are Biblical defenses against the Devil.

- fear him
- be aware of him
- resist him
- rebuke him
- fight him

II. Basic Training

How can *we* defeat the Devil? *We can't!* Ours is mainly a defensive posture; the battle is the Lord's. The Bible teaches that our attitudes are the key to success in this battle. We must heed the warnings of God's Word!

1. What attitudes must we adopt if we are to stand against Satan's attacks?

   2 Corinthians 2:11

   1 Peter 5:8

Second Corinthians 2:11 points out that we are not to be ignorant of the Devil's devices (thoughts, intentions). We must understand our enemy's aim.

The Lord Jesus declared that Satan is a murderer (John 8:44). What is a murderer? He is one who brings about death and destruction! Satan led Adam and Eve into sin, knowing that they would die physically and spiritually and that their relationship with God would be destroyed. Satan still operates the same way. He delights to see people die physically since they are a reflection of God's image. But more importantly, he works to bring spiritual death to as many as possible so they will suffer everlasting death and destruction (2 Thessalonians 1:8, 9).

2. What methods does the wicked one use to hinder unbelievers from hearing the truth of God's Word?

   Luke 8:11, 12

   2 Corinthians 4:3, 4

   2 Timothy 2:25, 26

If Satan fails to keep people from trusting Christ as Savior, his goal then becomes to render them ineffective for God. He will put his efforts into leading believers astray, keeping their lives unfruitful and their witness for Christ weak.

3. (a) How did Peter describe Satan in 1 Peter 5:8?

(b) When a lion seeks its prey, which animals in a herd will be most vulnerable to its attack?

(c) Bringing this principle to a spiritual level, what kinds of believers will Satan most successfully take down?

Not only should we be informed about Satan's aim, but we should be aware of his tactics. Ephesians 6:11 tells us to be prepared for attack. The more we understand his tactics, the more prepared we'll be!

Tactic #1: Instigating rebellion against authority. Just as Satan rebelled against God's authority over him, so he wants you to step out from under the authorities that God has placed over you.

4. In what ways did Satan tempt the people described in the following passages to step out from under authority?
     Genesis 3:1–6

     Luke 4:1–4

5. What authority figures does God often put into our lives? See Romans 13:1; Ephesians 5:22; Ephesians 6:1; Hebrews 13:7, 17.

Tactic #2: Planting sinful ideas. Satan wants to influence your thoughts to cause you to do sinful acts.

6. In the following passages, how did Satan influence these people's thoughts?

1 Chronicles 21:1–7

John 13:1, 2

7. Remember, Satan desires your spiritual downfall. He will provoke thoughts of guilt, doubt, fear, pride, and self-sufficiency to ruin you. Read Luke 22:31–34.

(a) What thoughts did Satan plant in Peter's mind that led to his fall?

(b) What was Satan looking to accomplish?

Tactic #3: Using lies and half-truths to deceive. Satan wants to spiritually confuse and disable you by causing you to think unbiblically. (Recall lesson 3!) He will even use Scripture verses out of context and twist the meaning to suit his purposes. (Consider Christ's wilderness temptation.)

Also, he is the source behind much of this world's "wisdom." He puts his lies and deceit into the mouths of his puppets. He can cloak his falsehood in intellectual snobbery, political correctness, and religious rhetoric. His persuasive arguments seem so logical and reasonable. Believer, be on your guard. Know truth!

8. Read 2 Corinthians 11:1–4, 13–15.
   (a) How did Paul describe the way Satan (the serpent) works (v. 3)?

   (b) What "lies" does Satan use to corrupt people's minds (v. 4)?

   (c) How is the Devil described (v. 14)?

   (d) What is one of the ways he spreads falsehood (vv. 13, 15)?

Tactic #4: Using the world and the flesh to seduce people into sinful living. Though in this study we've examined the world and the flesh as spiritual enemies in themselves, Satan will work through these to prompt you to sin. He knows that the flesh is our human frailty, and he will dangle worldly allurements (his to give [Luke 4:6]) to provoke us to sin through our fleshly lusts. Often he pinpoints a particular area of weakness to get us to fall.

9. What weakness can Satan use to lead us astray as cited in these passages?
   Acts 5:1–4

1 Corinthians 7:4, 5

1 Timothy 5:11–15

We're instructed in Ephesians 6:11 to put on the *whole* armor of God. If Satan can find a weak spot, he'll seek to gain a foothold. (The Greek word for "foothold" means "a place," "a room," "an opportunity.")

10. What is one such foothold, as recorded in Ephesians 4:26 and 27?

You've heard the saying, "Give him an inch, and he'll take a mile." Well, in Satan's case we might say, "Give him a foothold, and he'll build a fortress." If you give him a room in your heart, he'll begin to construct a castle there, a stronghold of sin. A stronghold is an entrenched sin, an area in which a believer sins repeatedly.

A believer who struggles with the stronghold of a besetting sin feels like a failure, constantly confessing and committing the same sin again and again. (Remember, Satan is also the accuser. It's just like him to provoke us to sin and then remind us of our failure and shame!)

11. How can you pull down a stronghold of sin? (Review questions 9–15 in lesson 5.) What instruction can you glean from 2 Corinthians 10:4 and 5?

Tactic #5: Sowing discord in relationships. Satan delights to sever relationships, destroy unity, and neutralize the effectiveness of God's people.

It pleases him to tear down the testimony of believers or tear apart the work of God in families, churches, or Christian outreaches.

12. Read John 13:35 and 17:21–23. What motivation does Satan have to sow discord among believers?

13. According to James 3:14–18, what kind of "Devilish" behavior will Satan sow among believers?

We've examined the intentions and tactics of the wicked one. What, then, is our defense against his attacks?

14. First, *be watchful* over your soul. Don't underestimate the enemy's desire for your downfall. What dangerous attitude can a believer have, as stated in 1 Corinthians 10:12?

15. Second, realize that *you can resist* the Devil. James 4:6–10 outlines several attitudes that enable us to do this. What are they?

16. Another way of resisting the enemy is by knowing God's Word. It is our mighty defensive weapon. When Christ quoted Scripture to counter Satan's temptations, what did Satan finally do (Matthew 4:11; Luke 4:13)?

17. We also resist Satan by prayer. Christ set the example in this as He prayed for His own to be kept from Satan's harassment (Luke 22:31, 32; John 17:15). How should we pray to withstand the Devil, according to Ephesians 6:18?

18. What words of assurance did Paul give believers regarding Satan in Romans 16:20?

Yes, we can resist the enemy! Put on the *whole* defensive armor God has given you. Know the Word, pray with perseverance, and guard your heart by humble attitudes. Don't give him a foothold in your life. Confess sin. Flee sources of temptation that he can use to provoke your fleshly lusts. Last of all, don't be a lone soldier! Recall that Satan attacks the isolated. A solitary soldier is more vulnerable than one in a battalion. Get into a Bible-teaching local church where you can grow in your knowledge of the truth, where you can be encouraged, and where you can gain a degree of spiritual protection (Hebrews 10:25).

III. Deployment

1. (a) Which of Satan's tactics do you most need to defend against? Why?
- Stepping out from under authority
- Being influenced by damaging ideas
- Being confused by lies, deceit, half-truths
- Falling into sin through weaknesses, footholds, and strongholds
- Allowing discord in relationships

(b) How might you defend against your vulnerability?

2. Though Peter fell when tempted, he did not fail in the faith. He repented, and the Lord Jesus restored and used him. When you are plagued by Satan's accusing thoughts of failure, with what Scriptural truth can you combat the Devil's condemnation?

3. How does Satan make sin seem acceptable, even beneficial?

4. Our enemy seeks to attack the defenseless young, the weak, the weary, the sickly, and the isolated.

(a) What can you do to be sure you are none of the above?

(b) How can you encourage those believers who may be vulnerable to the Devil's attacks?

IV. Debriefing

Consider the following questions, based on your study of this lesson.

- Do you understand Satan's aims and tactics?
- Are you vulnerable to his attacks?
- Have you allowed him to exploit weaknesses, gain a foothold, or build a stronghold in your life?
- Are you putting on the whole armor of God through His Word and prayer?

V. Battlefield Report

We are not commanded to fight the Devil or to fear him. The Scriptures give us no magical formulas or mystical ceremonies to keep Satan at bay. But this does not mean we are left wide open to his attacks. Don't give the enemy an opportunity to bring you down. Be on your guard! Put on your whole armor by the Word and by prayer. As you stand in God's grace and resist the Devil by faith, the enemy will be put to flight!

Our Captain and Commander

"But thanks be to God, which giveth us the victory through our Lord Jesus Christ" (1 Corinthians 15:57).

I T WAS a rag-tag army with unlikely prospects of victory. Yet the Continental Army was placed under the command of a Virginia farmer, George Washington. Constantly facing a superior opponent, a scarcity of food and supplies, and the severest of weather conditions, many soldiers were tempted to desert, and some did. But by his example of willing self-sacrifice, by his steadfast spirit of resolve to keep fighting, and by his concern and affection for the welfare of his troops, General Washington motivated his weary warriors and led them on to one of history's greatest triumphs!

An army may be skilled and brave. An army may have effective weapons. But without a commander, an army will falter against its foe. Troops without a leader will not understand their mission or feel secure of success. As Christian soldiers, we dare not go it alone. We must follow and obey our Captain and Commander.

I. Recruit Evaluation

As a believer, you have been enlisted into the Lord's army. But are you in the fight? How would you classify your current status in the spiritual conflict of life?

- I'm a deserter: I haven't been actively following Christ.
- I'm in the barracks: Though I'm doing my required "Christian routine," I'm taking it easy, spiritually speaking.

- I'm reporting for duty: I've been taking orders from my Commander and seeking to follow and obey Him.
- I'm on the front lines: I have been engaged in an intense, ongoing battle with the world, the sin in my flesh, and the forces of the Devil.

II. Basic Training

George Washington on his horse was said to be an imposing figure—an object of admiration and inspiration to his beleaguered troops. As believers engage in this persistent conflict, we look to our Lord and Savior Jesus Christ. He is worthy of our devotion and loyalty. He should be the object of our continual admiration and praise.

1. When our Lord revealed His power and glory, how was He described?

Matthew 17:1, 2

Revelation 1:13–16

2. According to Mark 16:19, where is He, bodily, at the present time?

As believers, we await the Rapture, Christ's return in the air to gather us to Himself and take us to Heaven (1 Thessalonians 4:16, 17). But at the end of the seven years of tribulation on earth, Christ will return to set up His Kingdom.

3. Read Revelation 19:11–16, which is the account of Christ's second coming, His return to earth.

(a) What will He be like at His coming to earth?

(b) Who will comprise the "armies of heaven" that accompany Him (Matthew 25:31; 2 Thessalonians 1:7; Jude 14, 15; Revelation 17:14; 19:14)?

4. (a) Now read 2 Thessalonians 1:7–10, which describes the same scene. What does this account tell you about the Lord?

(b) What will be our response to His victorious riding forth (v. 10)?

Yes, some future day our Commander will muster His heavenly army and ride forth to conquer all evil. What a day that will be!

But we dare not think that the battles are only in the future and that we can take our ease. No, our Master has a mission for us to accomplish now, and there are spiritual skirmishes to be fought and won. As the Captain of our salvation (Hebrews 2:10), Christ liberated us from the tyranny of sin and Satan. And now, dear sisters, you and I are called to be soldiers of Jesus Christ (2 Timothy 2:3). Your Captain and Commander wants you!

5. According to these verses, why should we be willing to follow and obey our Lord?

John 15:13, 14 (see also John 14:15, 21)

Galatians 1:4 (see also 2 Corinthians 5:14, 15; Titus 2:14)

6. What does our Lord ask of us if we are going to follow Him?
Matthew 16:24, 25

Luke 6:46–49

7. What "mission" does our Commander have for us? Read Matthew 28:18–20.

(a) What are His orders to us (vv. 19, 20)?

(b) What resource is available to help us carry out our mission (v. 18)?

(c) What promise did Jesus make to those who go out to fulfill His mission (v. 20)?

8. According to the following verses, what are some methods we must employ to accomplish our aim?
1 Peter 2:9, 10

1 Peter 2:11, 12

1 Peter 3:15, 16

9. As pointed out in the previous lesson, we are not instructed to personally take on Satan. However, we are told that we will "wrestle" (contend, struggle) against the powers of evil. As we declare God's praises, share the gospel, and witness boldly for Christ, how are we "attacking" Satan and his forces?

Acts 26:15–18 (see also Jude 23)

Ephesians 5:8–11 (see also Philippians 2:15, 16)

10. If we are supposed to be serving our Lord, how will He view us if we desert His ranks or take our ease? What qualities does the Lord expect from us as listed in 1 Corinthians 15:58?

11. First Corinthians 15:58 tells us that faithful service to our Lord is not in vain. How does God reward faithful service?

Hebrews 6:9–12

2 Peter 1:10, 11

2 Timothy 4:7, 8

Our love for Christ should motivate us to follow Him, obey Him, and serve Him. As we experience the battles of life, we can look to Him to protect us and lead us to victory.

12. What benefits are yours as a recipient of the care of your Captain and Commander?

Psalm 20:5–8

Psalm 34:4–7

Psalm 121

13. Why can we trust the Lord to deliver us in our spiritual conflicts? Does He have the power to do so? What claims did He make about His power over sin, the world system, and His enemy Satan?

John 8:34, 36

John 14:30 (see also 1 Peter 3:22)

John 16:33

14. Because Christ has prevailed, we will always prevail when, by faith, we abide in His victory. Read each reference below and explain how Jesus Christ is our victory in the various struggles of life.

1 Corinthians 1:24, 30, 31

1 Corinthians 15:55–57

2 Corinthians 2:14

Philippians 4:11–13

2 Thessalonians 3:3

III. Deployment

1. The apostle Paul often used military terminology to describe the Christian life. What similarities do you note between the requirements of a soldier's life and a believer's life?

2. A soldier's life is one of self-sacrifice. Yet, it seems that many of today's "Christian soldiers" are unwilling to sacrifice much or to be inconvenienced by their beliefs. In what ways have you had to "deny self" in order to be an obedient follower of Christ?

3. We understand our mission: to be lights for Christ in this dark world. Explain how doing each of the following will enable you to impact the unbelievers around you.

Declaring God's praises

Abstaining from worldly lusts

Displaying good behavior

Being willing and able to speak of Christ when people ask about your faith in Him

4. (a) The temptation could come to any of us to become a deserter or a slacker in our service to our Lord. If a Christian woman displays ungodly attitudes, unedifying speech, or unrighteous actions, who will be affected by her dishonorable conduct?

(b) How is such a woman disobeying the commands of Ephesians 5:8–11?

(c) In such a case, how does Satan gain a victory?

5. What attributes (qualities) of the Lord Jesus Christ are of comfort and strength to you in a battle you are facing right now?

IV. Debriefing

Consider the following questions, based on your study of this lesson.
- Is your heart filled with love, adoration, and praise for your Lord?
- Are you living a life of devotion, obedience, and self-sacrifice for Him?
- Are you seeking to be a witness for Christ to those around you?
- Are you looking to the Lord Jesus Christ to be your victory in the struggles of life you face?

V. Battlefield Report

"Follow Me!" The Lord Jesus gave that directive to many when He walked this earth. Some turned away. But others responded, left all behind, and followed Him.

At this moment, our living Lord is seated at His Father's right hand, having defeated sin, death, and Satan. He is the conquering Christ, and still He calls out to people, "Follow Me." He is enlisting a mighty army; He is sending us on a great, worldwide mission to make disciples. Are you faithfully following and fully obeying your Captain and Commander? Are you trusting in His victory as yours?

Defeats and Victories

"For whatsoever things were written aforetime were written for our learning, that we through patience and comfort of the scriptures might have hope" (Romans 15:4).

O N NEARLY every continent and in nearly every country, one may encounter war memorials and monuments to military heroes. The memorials remind us of the battles fought and the many lives lost in victory or defeat. Mankind seeks to remember those who have fought in years gone by and to learn lessons from both the glorious victories and the painful failures of the past.

As we read the Scriptures, we find in its pages records of glorious spiritual victories as well as accounts of painful failures. We discover that some men and women were heroes in their conflicts against the world, the flesh, and the Devil, while others fell in the fray. God has related to us their stories so that we will learn valuable lessons and face our conflicts with patience, comfort, and hope!

I. Recruit Evaluation

Which area of temptation do you think could most likely lead you to spiritual defeat?

- A love for the world's possessions and prestige
- Sexual sin
- A desire for money
- Pride, self-confidence, self-righteousness

II. Basic Training

First, let's examine the outcome of the lives of two men who were ac-
costed by the lure of the world. Which one was an overcomer and which
one was overcome?

1. Read the account of Demas in the following verses.
(a) In Colossians 4:14 and Philemon 23 and 24, what appears to
be the spiritual condition of Demas?

(b) What sad report of Demas did Paul give in 2 Timothy 4:10?
What cause is mentioned?

(c) According to Mark 4:18 and 19, how is a person like Demas
spiritually wounded by the world? (See also Luke 8:14.) What is the result?

2. In contrast to Demas, let's examine the life of Daniel. Read Daniel
5 and answer these questions.
(a) Describe the worldly power and possessions of Belshazzar
(vv. 1–4).

(b) In what ways did Belshazzar's power and possessions fail him
in this situation (vv. 5–9)?

(c) Describe the character and qualities of Daniel (vv. 10–12).

(d) What did Daniel have that Belshazzar, for all his worldly prestige, did not have (vv. 13–17)?

(e) What did the king offer Daniel (v. 16)?

(f) What was Daniel's response to his offer (v. 17)?

(g) What did God permit Daniel to receive from the doomed king (v. 29)?

3. Now read Daniel 6:1–5 and 11–23.

(a) Did the riches and position Daniel received from Belshazzar change his character? Explain.

(b) Did they divert his faith?

(c) Did the persecutions of the world break his faith?

4. As you compare the downfall of Demas with the victory of Daniel, explain how a believer may live *in the world* but not be overcome *by the world*.

Next, let's consider the lives of two believers who faced temptations of the flesh.

5. Read Genesis 39, the account of Joseph, who was sold into slavery by his jealous brothers.

    (a) What temptation of the flesh did Joseph face (vv. 7–10)?

    (b) How did the temptation come to him (v. 7)?

    (c) What justification might Joseph have given for giving in to temptation?

    (d) List at least three reasons Joseph gave for resisting the temptation (vv. 8, 9).

    (e) In what ways did the outcome of Joseph's situation seem like a defeat?

    (f) What words in the passage indicate that it was a spiritual victory (vv. 21, 23)?

6. Read 2 Samuel 11.

    (a) What temptation did David face (v. 2)?

    (b) How did the temptation come upon him?

(c) What reason did David have to resist temptation (v. 3)?

(d) What other sins did David commit to cover up his sin of adultery (vv. 13–21)?

(e) What words indicate that this was a spiritual defeat for David (v. 27)?

7. Read 1 Corinthians 10:12–14.

(a) How would you connect verse 12 to Joseph's and David's situations?

(b) How did Joseph escape his temptation?

(c) How could David have escaped his?

(d) How does verse 14 apply to these men's situations?

Last, let us look at the lives of two men who should have resisted the Devil. Both were defeated, but one was restored to hope!

8. Read Luke 22:31–34 and 54–62.

(a) What trial did Satan bring upon Peter that led to a defeat?

(b) What weakness do you think led to Peter's defeat?

(c) A clarification of verses 31 and 32, based on the Greek, would be, "Simon, behold, Satan hath desired you (all of you) that he may sift all of you as wheat. But I have prayed for thee (you, Peter), that thy faith fail not." Based on this, what do you think Satan's objective was in tempting Peter?

9. Read Luke 22:1–6.
(a) What did Satan use to tempt Judas to betray Christ? (See also John 12:4–6.)

(b) How was Judas's temptation different from Simon Peter's?

10. Read Matthew 27:3–5. Remember that Satan is a murderer (John 8:44). How did his tempting of Judas bring about Judas's death and destruction?

11. Now read John 21:1–19, which recounts Peter's restoration by the resurrected Lord.
(a) What indicates that Peter had not forsaken his faith in Christ (v. 2)?

(b) How do you detect that Peter is a repentant and changed man?

(c) What mission did the Lord have for His restored soldier (vv. 15–17, 19)?

12. Peter's life demonstrates that a believer may suffer some spiritual defeats yet ultimately walk in spiritual victory.

(a) What is the result, in Peter's view, of facing spiritual battles, as stated in 1 Peter 1:7?

(b) What is the "staying power" in our battles (v. 5)?

(c) What should be our attitude toward our testing times (v. 6)?

(d) What should be our focus (v. 7)?

III. Deployment

1. God permitted Daniel to receive material rewards and a position of influence. If God grants you such things, how can you be sure they don't corrupt your faith and take control of your heart?

2. Both Joseph and David were men of influence, but their thought patterns led them in different directions when tempted to sin. How do you suppose their thoughts were different?

3. Joseph suffered the misery of prison, a restriction of his outward freedom, but he had freedom of conscience. David suffered the inward misery of shame and guilt. David describes the agony of sin in Psalm 32. How can you find peace and forgiveness, based on his experience?

4. (a) Why may Satan seek to bring down those who lead others?

(b) How can you aid your leaders (fathers, husbands, pastors) in resisting Satan's attacks?

5. David was forgiven and restored in his fellowship with God. Peter went on to be a godly leader of the early church. Though they suffered temporary defeat, they were not utterly cast down. Explain what their lives teach you in the following areas.

Patience (endurance)

Comfort

Hope

IV. Debriefing

Consider the following questions, based on your study of this lesson.

- Can your heart refuse the riches and rewards of this world, or is it easily ensnared?
- Do you think through the perilous consequences of giving in to temptation? Or do you plan how to fulfill your desires once you have succumbed to temptation's pleasure?
- Do you know your particular weaknesses? Do you pray that you won't be led into temptation?
- Have you suffered a spiritual defeat that has paralyzed your walk with God?
- Will you confess your failure and accept God's forgiveness?

V. Battlefield Report

As you have served the Lord, you have no doubt experienced the thrill of victory and the agony of defeat. You've felt the joy as well as the shame and guilt. We all have!

David is an example of someone who had many moments of victory but also some devastating defeats. Yet, God called him "a man after his own heart" (1 Samuel 13:14), for God looked at the direction of David's heart over the course of his life. Though sin always brings consequences, God will restore and use us for His glory. What a gracious and merciful God He is!

Called to Conquer

"Nay, in all these things we are more than conquerors through him that loved us" (Romans 8:37).

Do you hear the bugle call? You are summoned to battle, sister in Christ. Are you engaged in this conflict against the wicked world system, Satan (the evil enemy of God), and the sinful forces of your own flesh? Perhaps you've been unaware that you have foes to face. Or maybe you've been wavering in your desire to wage war against these three. Should you choose to enlist, expect the war to be long and the battles to be intense. Put on your armor and ready your weapons. You've been called by your Captain to go forth and conquer. Forward, march!

I. Recruit Evaluation

How would you evaluate your current spiritual condition in the conflicts of life?

- I am discouraged; I feel weak.
- I am surrendering to the world/the weakness of the flesh/the Devil; I'm not fighting.
- I am watching, praying, and waging war.

II. Basic Training

1. What makes a good soldier? Note beside each verse the qualities of a commendable soldier.

1 Timothy 1:18, 19

1 Timothy 6:12–14

2 Timothy 4:7

Yes, we must remain faithful and finish the fight. But it isn't always easy to persevere when there is constant pressure and even pain. Paul encouraged Timothy to "endure hardness as a good soldier" (2 Timothy 2:3).

2. How do these passages encourage you to endure hardship?
James 1:12

1 Peter 4:1–7

1 Peter 4:12–19

When we are discouraged and downtrodden, weary and faint, we need to renew our strength (Isaiah 40:28–31). In lesson 2 we noted that our source of strength is the God of infinite power and might. David was a soldier who knew his Source of overcoming strength.

3. Read 1 Samuel 17:45–47. When David faced the fearsome giant Goliath, upon what did David depend for victory?

4. But David also experienced times of weariness and discouragement. What means did the Lord use to encourage David (1 Samuel 23:15–18; 18:1)?

5. At times God may use other believers to encourage us in our hard times. But sometimes we may find ourselves alone in the trenches of spiritual battle. David felt he had no one to turn to in the account recorded in 1 Samuel 30:3–6. What does verse 6 say he did?

How did David do that? David had a habit of talking to himself. When he felt down, he reminded himself of God's goodness and mercy.

6. Read Psalm 56.

(a) List several phrases that indicate that David was weary and discouraged.

(b) How did he talk to himself in a way that was spiritually encouraging (vv. 10, 11)?

Real life brings real difficulties: pressures, problems, opposition. Can we *really* conquer in the name of the Lord? We won't if we plunk ourselves in a rut of resignation and self-pity. When the going gets tough, the spiritually tough must get going! Consider the following account.

7. Read Nehemiah 4, the account of Nehemiah's efforts to rebuild Jerusalem's city walls.

(a) What kinds of opposition did Nehemiah and his people face (vv. 1–3, 7–9)?

(b) What was the mind-set of the people in these difficult circumstances (vv. 6, 21)?

(c) What was Nehemiah's primary plan of defense against the enemy (v. 9)?

(d) What other strategies did Nehemiah employ (vv. 16–20)?

(e) What was the foundation of Nehemiah's confidence that the Jews would prevail (vv. 14, 20)?

(f) What was the result of the enemies' efforts (v. 15)?

As we have seen in this study, we face pressures, problems, and opposi-
tions from the world, the sin in our flesh, and the enemies of darkness.
Hopefully, by now, you have seen through Scripture that you really can
prevail! God has provided both the resources and the promise of His power
so that we can experience the victory in our conflicts.

8. What Scriptural promises do we have that assure us of victory over
the world, the flesh, and the wicked one?
 Galatians 5:24

 1 John 5:4

 1 John 5:18

9. We are called to conquer! No matter what the battle, as we abide
in our Savior's life and love, we will triumph. Turn to Romans 8:31–39.
Beside each verse or set of verses, jot down the provision we have that
enables us to conquer in life's challenging circumstances.
 Verse 31

 Verse 32

 Verse 33

 Verse 34

Verses 35–37

Verses 38, 39

Some day our war will end, and we will at last rest from life's battles. At that future day, our Captain and Commander will reward his troops for their toil and trouble.

10. According to these verses from Revelation, what will be given to the overcomers?

2:7

2:11

2:17

2:26–28

3:5

3:12

3:21

III. Deployment

1. How have your Christian friends tried to encourage you during your times of hardship? Have they spiritually strengthened you?

2. How can you strengthen others in their battles?

3. When you become discouraged and overwhelmed, how do you encourage yourself in the Lord?

4. We can learn many lessons from the conflict presented in Nehemiah 4. Review the passage and answer the following questions.
   (a) When we are facing a difficulty or spiritual attack, why should prayer be our first response?

   (b) Why must we "set a watch" day and night for enemy attacks, as Nehemiah did?

(c) Reflect upon how the Jews worked together and fought the enemy together to build their wall (tools in one hand, swords in the other). How must Christians in a local church similarly work and stand guard together? What kinds of attitudes are needed to do this?

(d) We are called to do our part (watch, pray, work) and rely upon God to do His part. How will Satan's schemes be brought to naught as we do this?

5. So many wayward, weary, and wounded Christian soldiers are in our ranks! If God has promised us victory over the world, the sinful flesh, and the Devil, why do you think there are so many believers in a state of spiritual defeat?

IV. Debriefing

Consider the following questions, based on your study of this lesson.

- Do you have Christian friends who can encourage you when you are discouraged about life's conflicts? Do you make yourself accessible to them, or do you withdraw?
- Do you seek to strengthen others in their conflicts?
- Are you watchful and prayerful for your own spiritual well-being and for others'?

- Are you working and praying with other believers?
- Do you see yourself as a spiritual overcomer, trusting and fighting in the name of the Lord?

V. Battlefield Report

As women who belong to the Lord Jesus Christ, we will face spiritual battles every day. The attacks may come from without or within. The conflicts are genuine, and each battle you win or lose determines your spiritual condition now and for days to come. If you refuse to acknowledge that you are engaged in a real war, you are defeated already; that is just what Satan wants you to think.

An old Isaac Watts hymn asks some pointed questions:

> Must I be carried to the skies
> On flowery beds of ease,
> While others fought to win the prize,
> And sailed through bloody seas?
>
> Sure, I must fight if I would reign;
> Increase my courage, Lord;
> I'll bear the toil, endure the pain,
> Supported by thy word.

Are you conquering or being conquered? Are you surrendering to the world's bombardments? Are you succumbing to the sin in your own flesh? Are you being deceived by the Devil and his demons? Your Captain and Commander rallies you to His side! Don't be taken captive! With your God-given resources and weapons, battle it out in this long war. Your Lord has called you not only to fight but to conquer in His name and power. Dear sister-soldier, fight on!

LEADER'S
GUIDE

Suggestions for Leaders

The Bible is a living and powerful book! It is God speaking to us today. Every opportunity to learn from it is a precious privilege. As you use this study guide, be flexible. It is simply a tool to aid in the understanding of God's Word. Adapt it to suit your unique group of women and their needs. Use the questions as you see fit; the answers are provided to clarify my intent and stimulate your thoughts. You may have an entirely different insight as the Holy Spirit illumines your heart and mind.

Each section of the study has a specific purpose. The *introductory paragraphs* furnish background information and lead into the topic of that lesson.

The answers to the questions in *Section I* (Recruit Evaluation) are personal and should not be discussed in the group. They will help prepare each woman's heart to receive God's Word as she does her own study.

Section II (Basic Training) is aimed at studying the actual text of Scripture and understanding what it says.

The answers to the questions in *Section III* (Deployment) should help to focus on various applications of the passages for that lesson.

Section IV (Debriefing) is not for group discussion. The reflective questions are starting points for each lady to put God's truth into practice in her own life. You should close the session in prayer, asking God to bring lasting fruit from your study of His Word.

Section V (Battlefield Report) will help to seal in each lady's mind what she has learned from God's Word.

The effectiveness of a group Bible study usually depends on two things: (1) the leader herself; and (2) the ladies' commitment to prepare beforehand and to interact during the study. You cannot totally control the second factor, but you have total control over the first one. These brief suggestions will help you be an effective Bible study leader.

You will want to prepare each lesson a week in advance. During the week, read supplemental material and look for illustrations in the everyday events of your life as well as in the lives of others.

Encourage the ladies in the Bible study to complete each lesson before the meeting itself. This preparation will make the discussion more interesting. You can suggest that ladies answer two or three questions a day as part of their daily Bible reading time rather than trying to do the entire lesson at one sitting.

You may also want to encourage the ladies to memorize the key verse for each lesson. (This is the verse that is printed in italics at the start of each lesson.) If possible, print the verses on 3" x 5" cards to distribute each week. If you cannot do this, suggest that the ladies make their own cards and keep them in a prominent place throughout the week.

The physical setting in which you meet will have some bearing on the study itself. An informal circle of chairs, chairs around a table, someone's living room or family room—these types of settings encourage people to relax and participate. In addition to an informal setting, create an atmosphere in which ladies feel free to participate and be themselves.

You can plan your own format or adapt this one to meet your needs.

1½-hour Bible Study

10:00—10:30	Bible study
	Leader guides discussion of half the questions in the day's lesson.
10:30—10:45	Coffee and fellowship
10:45—11:15	Bible study
	Leader continues discussion of the questions in the day's lesson.
11:15—11:30	Prayer time

ANSWERS FOR LEADER'S USE

Answers are provided for Bible study questions. Answers for personal questions are not usually provided. Information inside parentheses ( ) is additional instruction for the group leader.

LESSON 1
Section II—1. (a) Satan. (b) God had instructed Adam not to eat the fruit from that tree. (c) The Devil assured Eve she wouldn't die (a lie) and that she would be like a god, knowing good and evil. (*Discuss:* Why did Satan want Adam and Eve to disobey God?)

2. (a) God stated that they now knew good and evil. (b) Before their disobedience, they had only known good. Evil entered into man's heart to mar the image of God's goodness. (See, for example, Matthew 7:11 and Luke 18:19.)

3. Sin entered the world. The result was death for all people.

4. They became afraid of God; they felt guilt and shame (compare Genesis 2:25 and 3:10); they passed blame; the woman would experience pain in childbirth; the man would have to labor hard to get food from a cursed earth.

5. There would be continual conflict (enmity) between the offspring of the woman and Satan and his "seed" (demons). But a promise is made that one of the woman's seed (note the word "his") shall crush the serpent's head, indicating defeat.

6. *Psalm 14:2, 3*—No one is good or righteous in God's sight. *Isaiah 59:2*—Our sin separates us from a holy God. *James 1:15*—Sin brings death upon all people. *Romans 1:18*—Disobedience brings God's wrath (future judgment).

7. *Romans 5:17–19*—Righteousness. *1 Thessalonians 4:7*—Holiness. (Look up the words "righteousness" and "holiness." What is the difference between the two?)

8. *Romans 5:6–10*—Jesus was to die for ungodly sinners and save us from God's wrath. *Galatians 1:3, 4*—Christ gave Himself for our sins and delivered us from the evil of this world. *1 Peter 2:24; 3:18*—He died to bear our sins and to enable us to live righteously before God.

9. *Hebrews 2:14, 15*—He destroyed the power that death had over all people due to sin and therefore foiled Satan's plan. *1 John 3:8*—He came to destroy the works of the Devil.

10. *John 3:16–18*—By believing in the Lord Jesus Christ, Whom God sent into the world to save us. *John 11:25–27*—By believing on Him. *Romans 10:9–13*—By believing in Jesus Christ with one's heart and calling upon the Lord to save from sin. (*Discuss:* What happens when a person refuses to put her trust in Christ? Read John 3:36 and 8:24.)

11. *Romans 4:5*—Our faith is counted for righteousness. *1 Corinthians 6:9–11*—God considers us washed (pure, clean), sanctified (set apart as holy), and justified (declared "not guilty" before God). *2 Corinthians 5:21*—We are made righteous before God.

12. God wants us to be holy in our manner of living (conversation) because God's children should reflect His character.

Section III—3. God's absolute purity from sin necessitates a separation from it. Hell is the eternal state of separation from a holy God. Since people's souls and resurrected bodies will live forever, then there must be a literal place where unforgiven sinners will dwell apart from God. Regarding God's justice, all sin must be punished. God cannot rightly ignore disobedience. If people will not accept Christ's substitutionary death as the punishment for their sin, then they must bear it themselves. Hell is the place of punishment for sin.

LESSON 2

Section II—1. *Psalm 138:3*—Strength comes as an answer to a cry to God. *Psalm 144:1*—The Lord is our strength. *Isaiah 26:4*—The Lord is everlasting strength. (*Discuss:* How do we access this strength according to Isaiah 26:4?) *Isaiah 40:29*—God gives strength to the weak.

2. The Holy Spirit. (Leader, if your ladies are not familiar with basic doctrine, you may want to give a brief explanation of the person and work of the Spirit.)

3. By believing in the Lord Jesus Christ as Savior.

4. *Luke 4:1, 2*—The Lord Jesus was filled with the Spirit as He went into the wilderness to be tested by Satan. *Acts 4:1–14*—Peter and John were filled with the Spirit as they withstood persecution and imprisonment. They were witnesses for Christ. *Acts 13:6–12*—Paul had to overcome the evil influence of a sorcerer and effectively share God's Word with a government official.

5. *Romans 8:2*—Bondage to sin and spiritual death. *Romans 8:15*—Fear and doubt about God's acceptance and love for us. *Romans 8:26, 27*—Weakness in prayer; not knowing how to pray according to God's will. *1 Corinthians 2:9–12*—A lack of spiritual understanding; He teaches us as we study the Word. *1 John 4:2, 6*—Spiritual errors and lies that might confuse us; He will expose false teaching to us as we seek God through His Word.

(Leader, look up the word "dynamic" and discuss with your group how the Spirit's power is dynamic.)

6. (a) We may grieve and quench the Spirit. (Acts 7:51 also uses the word "resist.") (*Discuss:* How do we grieve and quench the Spirit?) (b) According to Ephesians 5:18, we are simply to allow the Spirit to fill us. He is like a river that will flow within us (John 7:38), but we can dam up the river if we allow the dirt and debris of sin to accumulate in our lives (1 John 1:9).

7. (a) The Sword of the Spirit, the Word of God. (b) The Spirit is the One Who moved the human writers to record the inspired words. He is also the One Who illumines, or makes plain, the Word to our hearts.

8. With each suggestion from Satan, the Lord Jesus defended Himself from temptation by quoting Scripture and reassuring Himself of God's will. But He also cut down Satan's reasoning (offense). Finally, with no success, Satan retreated.

9. *Luke 22:31, 32*—We might pray that our faith would not falter. *Luke 22:39–46*— We can pray that we would not enter into temptation. (*Discuss:* What temptations did the disciples face at that time? Do we ever face those same temptations?) *John 17:15*—We could pray to be kept from the evil one. (*Discuss:* For whom could we pray these things beside ourselves?)

10. *Always*—At all times (1 Thessalonians 5:17), in every sort of situation and need. *With all prayer*—All kinds of prayer: private, public, long, short, personal, intercessory. *Supplication*—Requests for specific needs. *In the Spirit*—His Spirit directs our spirit as we pray. *Watching thereunto*—The Greek words suggest being alert, not falling asleep. Be alert to every situation that requires prayer. *With all perseverance*—Don't quit praying due to boredom, busyness, complacency, or lack of answers. *For all saints*—Each and all; everyone needs our prayers!

11. *Hebrews 4:15, 16*—The Lord understands our temptations; therefore, He is willing and able to help us. We may come boldly to Him and ask for grace and enabling when we have a spiritual need. *James 5:16–18*—We are told that fervent prayer works! The most ordinary saint of God can accomplish great results through prayer.

12. (a) The armor is called the armor of God. God provides all the pieces of our covering. (b) This armor will enable us to stand our ground in the evil day (when Satan tempts us).

13. *Romans 13:12*—Light. *2 Corinthians 6:7*—Righteousness. *Ephesians 6:14, 15*—Truth, gospel of peace, faith. *1 Thessalonians 5:8*—Faith, love, hope of salvation.

14. *Ephesians 6:16*—The shield of faith. *Ephesians 6:17*—The helmet of salvation.

15. *1 Corinthians 15:57*—God will always give us the victory. *2 Corinthians 2:14*—God always causes us to triumph in Christ.

Section III—1. Some suggested answers are busyness, a lack of interest, perceived inability to understand the Scriptures for oneself.

2. We must apply ourselves to learn the Word and then apply it to our lives (James 1:22). Then we can share what we have learned from the Word in our conversations, in cards and letters, or in teaching opportunities. Also, as we learn and memorize God's Word, we will begin to call it to mind as we face various situations in life. As we do all of this, we *will* grow in our proficiency.

4. *Light*—Exposes sin and drives off the works of darkness (Ephesians 5:8–13) and brings glory to God (Matthew 5:16). *Righteousness*—Fends off Satan's accusations because

we know we are justified by Christ's work on the cross (Romans 8:33, 34). It also counters wickedness by godly living (2 Timothy 2:22). *Truth*—Exposes Satan's lies and deceit that can confuse us and cause us to stumble. *Peace*—Removes doubts and fears that may separate us from God as we experience forgiveness and acceptance from Him (Romans 5:1; 8:8). *Faith*—Counteracts doubt that Satan plants in our minds as he did in Eve's (1 Corinthians 16:13). *Love*—Enables us to thwart Satan's evil attempts to sow discord and strife (1 Peter 4:8).

5. As we spend time each day in His Word and in prayer, we become mentally prepared and spiritually armed and protected for the battles we will face. We "put on" Christ, His grace and strength, to stand even as He did (Galatians 2:20; 2 Timothy 2:1).

LESSON 3

Section II—1. (a) We are commanded *not* to walk in vanity of mind. (*Discuss:* What did Paul mean by this expression, "vanity of their mind"? Who are the "other Gentiles" to which he refers?) (b) The results of walking (a habitual pattern) in vanity of mind are having a darkened understanding; being alienated from God; being spiritually ignorant and blind; being desensitized in feeling; exhibiting lasciviousness, uncleanness, and greed. (c) Christians are commanded to put off these "old life" characteristics by being renewed in the spirit of their minds. (*Discuss:* Why did Paul use the phrase "*in the spirit* of your mind"? Why is it necessary for believers' spirits to be involved in what goes on in their hearts and minds? See Romans 8:16; 1 Corinthians 2:10; Ephesians 2:1ff. The Spirit communicates God's will to believers' spirits.) (d) The result of being renewed in mind is that we will put on, more and more, the "new man" (the new creation, which will conform to Christ's image). Our practice will begin to measure up to our righteous, holy position.

2. (a) We are instructed not to be conformed, or molded, to this world (age). (b) We will be transformed (changed) by renewing (making new in quality) our minds. (c) We will be able to prove (discern) the will of God. In other words, as we think in new patterns, based on God's Word, we will gradually be changed into that true child of God who lives, not according to the world's way of thinking, but according to God's way of thinking.

3. *Proverbs 4:23*—The heart is the wellspring of our character and choices, therefore we must diligently guard what enters there. Allow nothing to contaminate! *Proverbs 23:7*—The thoughts that we think in our hearts determine what we are in our inmost being; i.e., what we think reflects our true character. *Matthew 12:33–35*—Jesus explained that what is "stored up" in the treasury of our hearts (by continual thought patterns) not only determines if our character is good or evil but also influences our words/actions (fruit).

4. *1 Corinthians 3:3*—A carnal mind; it is a mind-set that is self-centered and worldly. Such a mind doesn't consider things from God's viewpoint. *1 Corinthians 3:19, 20*—Vain imaginations; foolish, empty thinking that is devoid of the knowledge of God and does not acknowledge His existence or authority. This is the condition described in Ephesians 4:17–19. Note that the antidote is truth (Ephesians 4:21) and the acknowledgement of God (Psalm 2:10–12; Proverbs 3:6, 7). A believer who neglects to learn the truth of God can also be taken in by vain and deceptive thoughts. *2 Timothy 1:7*—A fearful, doubting mind; Romans 8:6 tells us that a spiritual mind brings life and peace. When we are convinced God loves us and cares for us, fear and doubt are removed.

5. *2 Corinthians 10:5*—We are to cast down vain imaginations in our minds and all thoughts that don't acknowledge God. We are to take *every* thought captive into obedience to Christ. *Philippians 4:8*—We ought to focus on the qualities named in the verse in any person or situation. We are usually prone to be negative and critical, so thinking this way takes a disciplined mind. *Colossians 3:2*—We are to set our affection (in the Greek this includes thoughts and will) on spiritual, not earthly (worldly) things. *1 Peter 1:13*—We are to "gird up the loins" of our minds. The phrase suggests wrapping a loose garment securely about the body in order to take place in activity. So then, we are to take control of restless, wreckless, cumbersome thoughts that hinder our spiritual living. We are to be single-minded about living the Christian life in light of Christ's return.

6. *Deuteronomy 11:18*—His Word was to be stored up in heart and soul and always in the forefront of their minds. *Joshua 1:8*—The Word was to be readily upon their lips and minds. It was to be meditated upon at all times. It would impact their lives and bring about spiritual success. (*Discuss:* What do you think brings about a lack of spiritual success in the lives of some believers?) *Psalm 119:11*—The Word should be hidden in the heart as a deterrent from sin. *Colossians 3:16*—We are to let the Word dwell (abide) in us richly (abundantly). (*Discuss:* How can music, as mentioned in this verse, aid us in thinking Biblically?)

7. *Psalm 56:3, 4*—Fear. The answer for fear is always faith (trust) in God. Meditating upon His attributes (such as His power and faithfulness) and His promises can ease our fears. (See also Psalm 46.) *Romans 8:33, 34*—Feelings of self-condemnation and guilt. Since we have trusted in Christ's cross work, we are justified and forgiven, and Christ is our intercessor before the Father (1 John 2:1, 2). *Ephesians 4:31, 32*—Anger, bitterness, or a reluctance to forgive. God has graciously and mercifully forgiven us though we are undeserving. *1 Peter 5:5, 6*—Pride. God requires and rewards humility.

8. *Psalm 119:6*—He did not have to deal with shame or guilt. *Psalm 119:28*—He found inner strength in times of trouble. *Psalm 119:45*—He experienced freedom from sin's bondage. *Psalm 119:49*—He had true hope. *Psalm 119:98*—He had wisdom. *Psalm 119:165*—He had real peace in his heart.

9. *2 Corinthians 3:17, 18*—God is changing us into the glorious likeness of His Son by the Spirit's power. *Ephesians 1:19, 20*—The same power that raised Christ from death is at work in our lives. *Ephesians 3:20*—God can do more than we can ask or think as His power works in us. *Philippians 2:13*—God is working in us to bring us into conformity with His will. (Leader, this is such a vital truth! Stress to your ladies that the Christian life is not gritting their teeth and trying to "do better" in their own strength. Their growth will occur as they, by faith, yield to God's work in their lives.)

Section III—2. Pray that the Lord will make you sensitive to these carnal ways of thinking. Post Philippians 4:8 as a reminder of how God wants us to think at all times. Also, learn to "talk to yourself" Biblically! When you find yourself thinking negatively, hypothetically (in a harmful way), impurely, covetously, etc., and the Spirit brings it to your attention that you're doing so, rebuke yourself and remind yourself of Scripture verses.

3. Post verses; take a few moments to pray; have a moment of worship as you look out the window; listen to edifying music; read a short devotional; share praises with your children or others.

6. (Leaders, in order to encourage each woman to answer honestly, it would be best not to discuss this question in your group setting.)

LESSON 4

Section II—1. *John 15:18, 19*—As believers, we no longer belong to the world system; Christ has chosen us *out of* this world. *James 4:4*—In this particular war, there are two sides: God and the world. If we become allies with the world, we are on the side that opposes God. For believers, this "friendship alliance" ought not to be! *1 John 3:1*—We are now children of God. Since the world doesn't know Him, it does not know us; we are aliens to them and, therefore, enemies.

2. The lust of the flesh, the lust of the eye, and the pride of life. (Leader, you may want to discuss more fully what these three phrases mean.)

3. *Genesis 3:5*—Wanting to be like gods. (*Discuss:* In what wrong ways do we try to be like God?) *2 Kings 17:15*—Wanting to be like the heathen (unsaved); worshiping their gods. *1 Corinthians 1:20*—Wanting to be thought wise by the world's standards. (*Discuss:* How are people indoctrinated by worldly wisdom in our age?) *1 Timothy 6:9*—Wanting to be rich. (*Discuss:* How do we see this obsession manifested in our culture?) *1 Peter 3:3*—Focusing on physical beauty and outward appearance.

4. Human glory withers very quickly. (Read also Psalm 49:16–20 and Psalm 73.)

5. *Proverbs 22:4*—True honor comes about by humility and submission to God. The world pushes the idea that pride, self-exaltation, and self-assertion will bring us the recognition we "deserve." *John 12:26*—Jesus declared that genuine honor comes from God, not men. It is obtained by serving, not by being served. It results from following Christ, not by being independent and unaccountable.

6. It is vanity, that is, emptiness. It doesn't fulfill. In fact, in the end, it became "vexation of spirit."

7. *Proverbs 23:5*—Riches are uncertain, so don't set your heart upon them. *Matthew 6:19, 20*—Wealth is "corruptible" and temporal. *1 Timothy 6:7*—Wealth cannot be taken to Heaven.

8. *Matthew 6:24*—You will try to serve two masters, but you can't. You will forsake your true Master. *1 Timothy 6:9*—You will fall into sinful temptations; you will become ensnared by your own foolish and hurtful lusts; you will damage yourself. *1 John 2:15*—A love for this world's offerings will drive the love of God from your heart. (*Discuss:* What should be a believer's mind-set toward riches? Refer to 1 Timothy 6:17–19.)

9. The care of this world can choke the Word from a woman's life. (The Greek word for "care" suggests distractions or anxieties.)

10. *Matthew 6:31–34*—The daily duty of obtaining food and clothing. These are basic needs that must be met, but we may allow them to become preoccupations of life. *Luke 10:38–42*—Being busy, carrying out the routines of life. Again, we each have responsibilities to fulfill, but when we become *driven,* we may abandon our time and attention for God.

11. Afflictions and persecution are attacks the enemy will use to cause us to fall away.

12. The world is anti-God and anti-Christ. Since we belong to God, the world will be against us too. The world will bring tribulation upon us, but Christ, our Master, has lived victoriously over the world system and in Him, so can we!

13. *Thoughts/attitudes*—Consider yourself blessed; rejoice; love your enemies; don't retaliate against their mistreatment of you; stay focused on your eternal reward; be kind-hearted and merciful. *Words*—Bless enemies; pray for them. *Actions*—Show forbearance; do good; give; show kindness.

14. (a) He refused to take his position as Pharaoh's son. (b) He passed them up, understanding that sinful living only brings pleasure for a short time. (c) The reproach of Christ; a willingness to suffer as one of God's people. (d) By faith, trusting in God. (e) He had his focus on the invisible God and believed in the ultimate heavenly reward (v. 26).

15. (a) Endure hardness (sustain affliction).(b) Entanglement with the affairs of this life. A good soldier stays spiritually focused in order to fulfill her mission (v. 2). (c) We can come before the throne of grace (pray) and ask for grace as we need it. Recall from lesson 2 that the Spirit imparts to us grace and strength.

Section III—1. Suggested answers: (c) God wants us to be humble as Christ was; Philippians 2:8, 9. (d) Riches and things don't satisfy; Ecclesiastes 5:10. (e) Real wisdom comes from knowing God and His Word; Proverbs 2:6. (f) Accumulating things doesn't fulfill; Ecclesiastes 5:11. (g) Living for pleasure yields a spiritually dead life; 1 Timothy 5:6. (h) We must cast our cares upon the Lord; 1 Peter 5:7. (i) Endure persecution with patience; James 5:10.

2. We may imitate the world in "worshiping its gods," such as celebrities, athletes, and millionaires. We may be drawn to its ungodly music and entertainment. We may dress or act like the world, so that we will be accepted by it. (*Discuss:* Is *everything* in the world wicked? How can we discern what we can accept or avoid? Read 1 Thessalonians 5:21 and 22.)

3. The same athlete who is cheered in one game may be booed in the next.

4. The Lord tells us that we should have a good testimony before the unsaved. (Matthew 5:16; notice that the glory should go to God, not to us.)

LESSON 5
Section I—All the answers are false.

Section II—1. The flesh is helpless to be or do good on its own. We are *spiritually depraved*, tainted by sin in all our ways. Any goodness we have or do must come from God as its source (Romans 3:12; Luke 18:19). (*Discuss:* Does spiritual depravity mean that unsaved human beings are as bad as they can be? By what means does God restrain evil in us and in the world?)

2. *Romans 7:22, 23*—It creates a war within us. Though we belong to Christ and our minds are being transformed by the Spirit and the Word, we may still allow ourselves to be taken captive by the sin that dwells within us. *Romans 8:7*—The carnal (flesh-controlled) mind will fight against God and His precepts. *Galatians 5:17*—The desires of the flesh are contrary to the desires of the Spirit. When we yield ourselves to the drives of our flesh, we will not do as the Spirit leads us. (Thus, we grieve and quench Him. See Ephesians 4:30 and 1 Thessalonians 5:19.) *1 Peter 2:11*—Fleshly lusts war against our souls.

3. Christ said the flesh profits nothing. It cannot produce spiritual life or growth.

4. A person "in the flesh" cannot please God.

5. *Galatians 6:7, 8*—A person who lives to continually please the flesh will reap destruction. *James 1:14, 15*—Lusts lead people into temptation. Giving in to temptation leads to sin. Living a life of sin leads to spiritual death.

6. *Romans 13:13*—Rioting (drunken revelry), sexual immorality, pleasure seeking, quarreling, envy. *Galatians 5:19–21*—Adultery, fornication, impurity, excessive indulgence, idolatry, witchcraft, hatred, contention, evil intent, angry outbursts, self-centeredness, division, and unrestrained behavior. *Ephesians 5:3–5*—Fornication, uncleanness, covetousness, filthiness, foolish talking, obscene speaking.

7. *Matthew 6:1, 2*—Giving money to the poor or to God's work and doing it in such a way that others will know of it and think highly of the giver. *Matthew 6:5–7*—Praying before others in a way that causes them to take note of how "spiritual" the individual is. *Matthew 7:21, 22*—Being involved in "Christian" work or service without having a true faith relationship with Jesus Christ. (Some people may talk the talk and even walk *some* of the walk in their own flesh. But they lack true union with Christ as in John 15.)

8. *1 Corinthians 3:1–3*—Envy, strife, and division were evident in the Corinthian church. *1 Corinthians 6:1–8*—Believers were involved in disputes and going to civil court against one another. Paul implied that cheating was taking place. (*Discuss:* What would Spirit-filled Christians do if cheated rather than sue each [see verse 7]?) *1 Corinthians 11:17–22*—They weren't treating each other well at church gatherings. There were divisions. The Lord's Supper was turning into a gluttonous, drunken feast for some. The "have-nots" were being treated contemptuously by the "haves." *James 4:1–3*—Fighting, quarreling, selfishness, and covetousness. (*Discuss:* In what ways might these same problems still distress Christian families and churches?)

9. *Verses 2, 11*—You are dead to sin. *Verses 7, 18, 22*—You are freed from sin. *Verse 14*—Sin does not have dominion (or lordship) over you.

10. *Verse 6*—You are not to serve sin. *Verse 12*—You are not to let it reign in your body or obey it. *Verse 13*—You are not to yield your members (bodily parts) to sin, to be its instruments.

11. Jesus Christ our Lord. (Note that it is "Who" shall deliver us, not "what." The answer to our sin problem is a person, Jesus Christ. Also, He does not *help* us overcome sin but *delivers* us from our sinful flesh.)

12. "Yield yourselves." In order to yield ourselves, we must desire to do it and then act upon that desire.

13. *1 Timothy 6:9–11*—Flee temptations that stir up foolish and hurtful lusts. (*Discuss:* What particular temptation does Paul warn Timothy about in these verses? How can we flee that temptation?) *2 Timothy 2:22*—Flee youthful lusts. *1 Peter 2:11*—Abstain (keep a distance) from fleshly lusts.

14. (a) Walking in the Spirit. (b) Being led of the Spirit. (c) Love, joy, peace, longsuffering, gentleness, goodness, faith, meekness, and temperance. (d) The flesh will be "crucified" to us. The Spirit's power is able to deaden the effects of the flesh. (Read Romans 8:13, 14.) The Spirit grants us the freedom to live as children of God.

15. "Put ye on" the Lord Jesus Christ. (The idea in the Greek is "as sinking into a garment.") As we wrap ourselves in Christ—in mind, heart, and faith—we will find Him living out His life through us (Galatians 2:20) and bringing death to the lusts of the flesh in us.
Section III—1. "Works of righteousness which we have done" come forth from the flesh. The flesh profits nothing, nor is it pleasing to God. He will not accept our good works as payment for sin.

2. True believers may serve to feel self-righteous or achieve admiration from others. Since this is pride, it is a lust of the flesh.

3. Some carnal sins we condemn are adultery, fornication, involvement in pornography, or gambling. Sins we seem to accept are gossip, covetousness, pride, and bitterness.

4. Some sins offer temporal pleasure, and the pull of our lusts is very strong. We don't see ourselves as slaves of sin. The desires of the moment may take precedence over the long-term joy of holiness.

5. *Persons*—Those who entice us to sin (Proverbs 1:10; 4:14), to waste our money, to covet, or to compromise our testimony. *Places*—Bars, nightclubs, casinos, unedifying entertainment centers, perhaps even malls (if you struggle with covetousness). *Things*—Computers (if they are a source of temptation), ungodly TV programs, certain books or magazines, catalogs, lottery tickets, alcohol, tobacco.

6. By spending time with Him through the Word and prayer and continued meditation. We must look to Him continually by faith.

LESSON 6
Section I—All the answers are (b).
Section II—1. (a) He calls them principalities and powers. (The Greek words mean "rulers and authorities.") In some of these verses, Paul may be referring to earthly rulers or to both earthly and heavenly rulers. In other verses, he specifies them as rulers in the heavenly places. (In Ephesians 6:12 "high places" means heavenly realms.) (b) Angels.

2. Christ created all things including the invisible heavenly beings.

3. *Psalm 103:20, 21*—They excel in strength; they do God's commandments and all He says (they don't sin); they worship and praise God. *Luke 20:34–36*—Angels do not die, neither do they marry. *Hebrews 1:13, 14*—They are ministering (serving) spirits. (In the Old and New Testament periods, they acted as messengers or ministered to physical and emotional needs, as in Matthew 4:11 and Luke 22:43.)

4. *2 Peter 2:4*—They sinned. These angels likely participated in the rebellion of Satan against God and are no longer allowed to *dwell* in the heavenly realm. They now seem to roam about the earth and sky, though some have already been sent to Hell (2 Peter 2:4; Revelation 12:3–9). *Jude 6*—Though interpretations of this verse vary, the idea is that these angels stepped out of bounds. They were discontent with the position God had given them, wanting greater prestige and power.

5. *Matthew 12:22*—They can afflict people with bodily infirmities (Job 2:7). *Matthew 17:14–18*—They can inflict people with forms of insanity, even to the point of suicidal behavior. *Acts 16:16*—Demons are the power behind forms of witchcraft, divination, fortune telling, and other occult practices. Demons can pretend to be spirits of dead people for such purposes. (*Discuss:* What practices that seem innocent should be avoided by believers?) *1 Corinthians 10:20*—Demons are the true recipients in all idol worship and false worship. (That's why Jesus instructed us to worship in spirit and in truth.) *1 Timothy 4:1*—They influence people to believe false doctrine and heresy. *Revelation 16:14*—They can do miracles and impart to individuals the ability to perform signs and wonders. (See Matthew 24:24 and 2 Thessalonians 2:8, 9 for instance.) Their intent is spiritual deception. (*Discuss:* Knowing this, why should we be cautious about what we receive and believe as spiritual input?)

6. *1 Corinthians 6:19*—Believers' bodies are the "temple of the Holy Ghost." The Holy Spirit will not share His dwelling with a demon. *1 John 4:4*—"Greater is he that is in you, than he that is in the world." *1 John 5:18*—"That wicked one toucheth him not."

7. *1 John 3:8*—He sinned from the beginning. *1 Timothy 3:6*—He was lifted up with pride.

8. *Matthew 13:19*—The wicked one. *John 8:44*—He is a murderer and a liar. *John 12:31*—The prince of this world. *2 Corinthians 4:4*—The god of this world (age). *Ephesians 2:2*—The prince of the power of the air; the spirit that works in the children of disobedience. *1 Thessalonians 3:5*—The tempter. *1 Peter 5:8*—Our adversary; he's a roaring lion seeking prey. *Revelation 12:9, 10*—Great dragon, old serpent, the Devil (accuser), the deceiver of the whole world.

9. A heavenly army with chariots and horses of fire. (Read also Genesis 32:1, 2.)

10. (a) One who was sent from Heaven with a message for Daniel; an angelic messenger. (b) The "prince" (or ruler) of the Persian kingdom tried to thwart his coming to Daniel. This appears to be one of the "principalities." (c) Twenty-one days. (d) Three weeks (or twenty-one days). (*Discuss:* What might be the connection between the length of time Daniel faithfully prayed and the length of time the angel spent overcoming the demonic hindrances?) (e) Michael, the prince (or ruler) who defends the nation of Israel (Daniel 12:1). (Leader, for another example of demonic hindrance, read 1 Thessalonians 2:18.)

11. (a) Into the Lord's presence; up and down in the earth. (b) To afflict Job with loss, misery, bodily ailments. (c) Kill him. (d) The Lord God.

12. (a) He came to know God better; he became more humble. (b) God revealed Himself to these men; He demonstrated that His power ultimately was greater than Satan's. (c) Satan's accusation was that Job only worshiped God to get "blessings." When God permitted Satan to remove all the blessings, Job still believed in God and worshiped Him. Through the perseverance of a sinful mortal, God both rebuked Satan and his horde and demonstrated to them that He is worthy to be worshiped solely because of Who He is!

13. (a) The host of Heaven. (b) The spirit appears to be an evil spirit; he was a "lying spirit" in the mouth of the false prophets. Demons lie and deceive. (Note that God didn't tell the spirit to do evil; the spirit offered to do it.) (c) To persuade King Ahab to go to war. The king had wickedly rebelled against God for many years and by believing his false prophets, he would go to his death. It was God's will to bring Ahab's life to a close.

14. *Daniel 7:13, 14*—The Son of Man Who is given dominion, glory, and an everlasting kingdom. *Matthew 25:31–34*—He is the Son of Man Who sits upon the throne as king. *Revelation 19:16*—He is the King of Kings and Lord of Lords. (Leader, remind your ladies that when Jesus walked the earth, demons were always subject to Him and could not resist His will.)

15. *John 12:27–33*—By the death He died on the cross, He judged and defeated Satan. He triumphed over sin and Satan by providing salvation for mankind's sin. *Hebrews 2:14*—Christ destroyed the power of death and of the Devil by His own death.

16. *Revelation 12:7–9*—Satan and his army will be cast out of the heavenly realms and allowed to stalk only the earth. *Revelation 20:1–3*—He will be cast into the Bottomless Pit for a thousand years. *Revelation 20:7–12*—He will be cast into the Lake of Fire forever.

Section III—1. Many suppose angels to be the spirits of dead people who have returned to this world to guide and protect others. In their thinking, cherubs are babies who have died. These views are unscriptural. Angels do not persuade people to live a better life, either.

2. Angels probably protect us at times from physical danger. They might also "fight back" evil influences that demons might seek to bring upon us. In the world, they are fighting off the "principalities" that seek to hinder God's work. They also carry out God's instructions.

3. We are always kept in the love of God. We have been given resources to be able to stand against the forces of evil; we are not powerless. The Holy Spirit is greater than Satan. We have overcome Satan by the blood and name of Christ. Demonic powers are always subject to the will of God.

4. We should view demonic activity as being real. We should be careful about what we expose ourselves to, as demons seek to deceive. We should, above all things, pray as Daniel did, so we can do our part to deter the forces of evil.

LESSON 7

Section I—We are never told to fear him, rebuke him, or fight him. We are told to be aware of him (1 Peter 5:8) and to resist him (James 4:7).

Section II—1. *2 Corinthians 2:11*—We must be informed, not ignorant, of his intentions toward us or he will get an advantage over us. *1 Peter 5:8*—We are to be sober (serious) and vigilant (watchful). God wants us to take our enemy seriously and be on our guard.

2. *Luke 8:11, 12*—Satan snatches the Word from people's hearts. (*Discuss:* By what means do you think Satan snatches the Word from people's hearts?) *2 Corinthians 4:3, 4*—He blinds people's minds to the truth of the gospel. Consider the Pharisees who had God walking in their very midst! *2 Timothy 2:25, 26*—Satan takes people "captive" by their sin so that they won't repent and receive God's truth.

3. (a) Satan is described as a roaring lion seeking prey. (b) Most vulnerable to a lion's attacks are the undefended young, the weak, the sickly, the isolated, or the weary. (c) Satan will attack new believers who do not have a good support system, those who fall easily into sin and doubt, those who are not well grounded in sound doctrine, those who do not attend church, and those who might be worn down by stress and trials. (*Discuss:* As you read 1 Peter 5:9 and 10, in what category did Peter seem to consider the believers to whom he was writing?)

4. *Genesis 3:1–6*—He tempted Eve to step out from under God's authority as well as her husband's authority as the head of the family. (*Discuss:* What was Satan's motive as subtly stated in verse 5? What does being under authority teach us that Satan doesn't want us to learn?) *Luke 4:1–4*—Satan tempted the Lord Jesus to use His power to provide for His own needs rather than trusting and depending upon His Father to meet them.

5. Everyone is to submit to the civil authorities; children are to obey their parents (adult children are to honor them); wives are to submit to their own husbands; believers are to submit to church leaders who teach the Word and watch over their souls. (*Discuss:* How does being a part of a local church offer us a degree of spiritual protection against the forces of darkness? See, for example, 1 Corinthians 5:5 and 1 Timothy 1:20.)

6. *1 Chronicles 21:1–7*—Satan provoked David to take a census of Israel and its army, an act that was seemingly motivated by pride or insecurity. God had not instructed David to do this and was displeased by the act. The king was to trust God for security, not his army.

John 13:1, 2—Judas was under the influence of Satan in his betrayal of Christ.

7. (a) Thoughts of pride, self-confidence. (b) He wanted Peter to fail and fall away from the faith. Perhaps he figured Peter would be too filled with shame and guilt to continue as a disciple.

8. (a) He beguiles (deludes, deceives) by subtilty (guile, cunning, trickery); he corrupts people's minds. (b) The preaching, or setting forth, of "another Jesus," "another spirit," or "another gospel." (*Discuss:* In what forms do we observe this tactic today?) (c) An angel of light; that is, he can disguise himself in "Christian" form, seeming to do good. (d) Through false messengers of Christianity. They use Christian rhetoric but deny the true power and message of Biblical Christianity. (See Matthew 7:21–23; 2 Peter 2:1, 2; 1 John 4:1–3; 2 John 7–11.)

9. *Acts 5:1–4*—He filled the hearts of Ananias and Sapphira to lie about how much they were giving of the land that they sold. The area of weakness Satan exploited seemed to be a desire for recognition among believers or perhaps envy (of Barnabas and others; Acts 4:34–37). *1 Corinthians 7:4, 5*—If a husband or wife denies the spouse sexual relations, that mate may be tempted to commit adultery. *1 Timothy 5:11–15*—Young widows apparently struggled with loneliness, and Satan was luring them into ungodly behavior, sexual sin, and perhaps even marrying unbelievers.

10. Being angry with a person. (*Discuss:* How can being angry with someone give Satan a foothold in your life?)

11. We are to remember and depend upon our spiritual weapons: the Spirit's power at work in us, the Word of God, prayer, and our identification with Christ. A stronghold can only be brought down by the mighty power of God in us through all these things. *We are responsible* to cast down imaginations (those thoughts that lead to sin) and any thinking that is contrary to God's will. Every thought must be brought captive to Christ, as thinking determines behavior.

12. The love and unity of a body of believers is a testimony to the deity, power, and love of Christ.

13. Bitter envy, strife, confusion (disorder), and every sort of evil behavior.

14. Overconfidence—an attitude that we could never be tripped up by Satan. (Remember Peter!)

15. We should humbly seek to stay close to Him; be serious about having a holy life; and submit gladly to His will instead of being stubborn, proud, and resistant. We're actually told here that as we do these things, Satan *will flee from us!* Amazingly, a humble, faith-filled, sensitive believer is the spiritual warrior Satan can't overcome! (Read 1 Peter 5:5–10 for a parallel passage.)

16. He departed; he left Him alone.

17. Pray always; pray all kinds of prayers; pray in the Spirit; pray and be watchful; pray with perseverance; pray for all saints. (*Discuss:* Why does Satan try to hinder us from spending time in prayer? Is he succeeding?)

18. God will soon bruise Satan beneath out feet!

Section III—2. Recall that Peter was forgiven and restored by Christ. Meditate on such verses as Romans 8:34; 2 Timothy 2:13; 1 John 1:9; and 2:1.

3. Satan plants ideas in our minds that cause us to excuse our sin, such as "It's not really hurting anyone," or, "Everyone does it." He has influenced the world to "whitewash"

sin by using words that don't sound as bad (not adultery, but an extramarital relationship; not homosexuality but alternative lifestyle, etc.) He has used the media and educational institutions to "preach" tolerance of sin.

4. (b) We can encourage believers to come to church, Bible study, or other church-related events. We can also share what we have learned from the Word.

LESSON 8

Section II—1. *Matthew 17:1, 2*—When His glory is revealed, His face shines as the sun and His clothes are glistening white. *Revelation 1:13–16*—He wears a golden sash about His body; His hair is snowy white; His eyes are like flaming fire; His feet are like polished brass, and a double-edged sword comes out of His mouth.

2. He is seated at the Father's right hand. (*Discuss:* What does being at "the right hand" signify?)

3. (a) He will be riding on a white horse to judge the earth and make war. He will reveal His power by His flaming eyes and His many crowns. He will be wearing a vesture sprinkled with blood, and again, a sharp sword will come out of His mouth. Thus will He lead forth the armies of Heaven. (b) The armies of Heaven are comprised, seemingly, of angels and the glorified believers who were previously raptured (the glorified Church).

4. (a) He will return in flaming fire and with vengeance upon the ungodly. He will come in a display of glorious power. (b) We will admire Him and glorify Him.

5. *John 15:13, 14*—He loved us and laid down His life for us; therefore, we should show our love to Him through obedience to His commands. *Galatians 1:4*—He gave Himself for our sins; He delivered us from the evil world system; He redeemed and purified us. Therefore, we should no longer live for ourselves but for Him.

6. *Matthew 16:24, 25*—He expects us to deny self, lose our lives for His sake. We are signing on for a difficult, yet fulfilling and abundant, life. *Luke 6:46–49*—If we call Him our Lord, we must do as He says. Obeying Him brings us stability.

7. (a) We are to go and make disciples for Christ and teach them to obey and follow Him. (b) The power of Christ. He has all the power of Heaven and earth at His disposal to give to us as we go. (c) He will always be with us.

8. *1 Peter 2:9, 10*—We are to declare God's praises and mercies to the unsaved people around us. (*Discuss:* How do we do this tactfully?) *1 Peter 2:11, 12*—We're to abstain from fleshly lusts, showing that our lives are focused on something more beneficial and fulfilling. We are to display integrity so that we'll have a blameless testimony for Christ. *1 Peter 3:15, 16*—We are to be willing and able to speak to others who may ask us about our faith in Christ. Our good behavior must back up the things we declare.

9. *Acts 26:15–18*—When a person receives Christ, he or she is snatched out of Satan's power and the jaws of Hell. When you play a part in a person's salvation, you are participating in thwarting Satan's objective. *Ephesians 5:8–11*—We expose the works of darkness as we "shine our light" upon them.

10. He requires us to be steadfast and immovable in our faith, always working diligently to do His will in the world.

11. *Hebrews 6:9–12*—He will not forget our faithful service done out of love for Him. (*Discuss*: This passage warns us not to be slothful, but diligent. What will cause a woman to become lazy about serving Christ? What are the symptoms of such laziness?) *2 Peter 1:10,*

11—The idea expressed in verse 10 is "Live in such a way that demonstrates that your salvation is a real thing." In other words, be faithful so that you can be *joyfully* received into Heaven by the Lord. *2 Timothy 4:7, 8*—Those who have fought the good fight and long to see their Captain and Commander receive a crown of righteousness!

12. *Psalm 20:5–8*—We can stand in the name and power of the Lord. *Psalm 34:4–7*—The Lord will deliver us from all our fears and out of all our troubles. *Psalm 121*—The Lord is our keeper; He never sleeps. He will preserve us from all evil.

13. *John 8:34, 36*—He can free people from the bondage of sin. *John 14:30*—He is not subject to Satan, the prince of this world. Satan has no power over Him. *John 16:33*—He has overcome the world.

14. *1 Corinthians 1:24, 30, 31*—Christ is our source of power and wisdom and the One through Whom we have righteousness, sanctification, and redemption. He provides all we need for our salvation. *1 Corinthians 15:55–57*—He is the one Who gives us victory over sin and death. *2 Corinthians 2:14*—As soldiers in His army, we are part of His triumphal procession as we go through this world. *Philippians 4:11–13*—In all the ups and downs of life, He can strengthen us to be content. *2 Thessalonians 3:3*—He is faithful to establish us and keep us from evil.

Section III—1. A soldier is under the complete authority of those in command; a believer is under Christ's authority. A soldier must be disciplined, brave, and endure hardship; so must we. A soldier must obey unquestioningly; we must also obey fully and immediately.

3. As we praise God, we draw attention to the fact that *He is* (Hebrews 11:6) and that we acknowledge His control over all of life. By abstaining from fleshly lusts, we show that He has given us victory over sin (with which unbelievers struggle) and that we live for a higher purpose than to "eat, drink, and be merry." The good behavior of controlled attitudes, gracious and edifying words, and loving, patient actions demonstrates a difference of life. As unbelievers inquire about that difference, we should be willing and able to tell of Christ's sacrifice for sin and how He can make a difference in their lives.

4. (a) First, the Lord will be dishonored because she has claimed His name (2 Timothy 2:19). Then, she not only affects her own life (stagnation sets in; see 2 Peter 1:5–9), but she cannot spiritually impact those around her (family, friends, coworkers, neighbors). (b) If she is a "neutral" witness, she can't reprove the works of darkness. Her light is dim! (c) She is one less believer who is standing against the works of darkness. She poses no threat to aid in the deliverance of a soul from Hell. That's Satan's objective!

LESSON 9

Section II—1. (a) Demas was a believer, a fellow worker in the gospel with Paul and other servants of Christ. He was ministering to Paul during Paul's imprisonment in Rome. (b) Demas had forsaken him in Paul's time of need and had gone to Thessalonica. Paul indicates that a love for the world caused Demas to leave. (c) The world inflicts spiritual damage by its cares, riches, and desires that enter into the heart and choke out the Word. The result is an unfruitful life.

2. (a) He had power over a kingdom and a thousand lords. He could indulge his fleshly appetites with feasting, wine, and wives. He had riches (including gold and silver vessels taken from the Lord's temple). (b) They couldn't make him wise, answer his problems, or remove his fears. They couldn't humble his heart and make him right with God, nor could they save

his kingdom from defeat. (c) Daniel was esteemed for having wisdom and understanding. He was regarded as a man of integrity. (d) Daniel had peace with God in his heart and the assurance of God's favor. (e) Scarlet clothing, a gold neck chain, a position as the third ruler in the kingdom. (f) Daniel refused them. Basically he said, "Keep your gifts and give your rewards to someone who wants them!" (g) The very things Daniel refused were given to him anyway. (*Discuss*: Why do you think God allowed Daniel these things?)

3. (a) Daniel was still the same man of knowledge, excellence, and dependability. (b) Daniel was still strong in his faith, a man of prayer and devotion to God. (c) No, even in the face of death, he was faithful.

4. Both Demas and Daniel lived in the world, but Daniel's heart was so grounded in his faith in God that neither riches nor persecution could move him away from the Lord. Demas's heart, however, became ensnared by the world, and he forsook the Lord's work.

5. (a) Joseph faced the temptation of sexual sin. (b) The wife of his master kept trying to seduce him. (c) Joseph was a stranger in a foreign land ("No one will know I worship God."); he had endured great personal adversity ("I deserve a little fun after all I've been through!"); he was in a pagan culture where such sins were common ("Everyone does it."); no one was around ("No one will know!"). (d) "My master trusts me" (v. 8); "I'll ruin my reputation and lose my position" (v. 9); "You're *his wife*" (v. 9); "This would be wicked" (v. 9); "I would be sinning against God—He'll know!" (v. 9). (e) He ended up in a dungeon though he had done nothing wrong. (f) "The LORD was with Joseph," "shewed him mercy," "gave him favour," "the LORD made it to prosper." In other words, God was pleased with Joseph's resolve and integrity.

6. (a) David faced the temptation of sexual sin. (b) He was taking in some air on his palace roof when he saw from afar a beautiful woman bathing. David proceeded to inquire about her (v. 3), send for her (v. 4), and sin with her (v. 4). (*Discuss*: Verse 1 mentions that kings were expected (in the spring) to head out and fight the enemy. But David *took his ease* [recall lesson 8] and let others fight the battle. How can neglect of responsibilities or having too much free time lead a woman into temptation?) (c) By God's grace David had been given a position of leadership, privilege, and responsibility. Bathsheba was another man's wife, as David well knew (v. 3). David had plenty of wives to satisfy his needs (2 Samuel 3:2–5; 5:13). (d) He tried to cover up Bathsheba's pregnancy; he made Uriah get drunk; he orchestrated Uriah's death. (e) "The thing that David had done displeased the LORD."

7. (a) Joseph took heed to his position of peril. He fled temptation so he would not fall. David lingered at Jerusalem, seemingly secure in his past victories and all that the Lord had done for him. In his moment of false security, he fell. (b) He understood that it would be his ruin (Proverbs 6:32). He refused to listen to her words (Proverbs 5:3, 4) or go near her (Proverbs 5:8). Finally, he "got him out!" (*Discuss*: When might a believer have to "get out" of a situation to overcome temptation or sin?) (c) David could have avoided the opportunity to sin if he had been where he was supposed to be (with his troops). He also could have refused to mentally dwell upon what his eyes had seen. He could have gone to one of his own wives to fulfill his desires. He could have reminded himself that Bathsheba was another man's wife. He should have said what Joseph said: "How then can I do this great wickedness, and sin against God?" (d) Any person or thing that we desire more than God is an idol. Paul warned us to flee idolatry. For David, Bathsheba became an obsession, an idol.

8. (a) Satan brought Peter into contact with people who asked if he was a disciple of

Jesus. Out of fear for his life, Peter denied knowing Him. (*Discuss*: Some people wonder if Peter denied the faith and fell from grace. Did Peter deny that Jesus was Messiah or deny *knowing* Him? Did he reject *the way of salvation* or tell a lie?) (b) Seemingly, Peter was proud of his position of leadership among the disciples (Mark 14:26–31) and perhaps considered himself more spiritual and loyal. His weakness might have been that he didn't think he had a weakness! (c) Satan wanted Peter to fall away from the faith (through guilt, shame), and then perhaps the others would as well. Peter *was* the leader (as we come to see in the book of Acts), and he had great influence.

9. (a) Money. (b) Whereas Satan attacked Peter's weakness of pride, he attacked Judas's weakness of greed. Satan *harassed* Peter, who was a believer, but he *possessed* Judas (Luke 22:3), who was an unbeliever. Peter's sin came in a moment of fleshly weakness (fear), while Judas's sin was a premeditated act.

10. Satan planted thoughts of guilt and shame in both Peter's mind and Judas's mind. But while Peter turned back to his Lord, Judas turned to suicide and damnation.

11. (a) Even after denying Christ, Peter sought to be with the other disciples. (b) The self-confident pride was gone. He no longer boasted but humbly said, "Lord, thou knowest all things." He refused to use the word "agape" (unconditional, godly love) but used "phileo" (brotherly love) in recognition of his own fleshly weakness. He no longer trusted himself, and that was a good thing! (*Discuss*: Why would Peter be a better leader after his defeat than before?) (c) To follow Him and feed His sheep (make disciples and teach them).

12. (a) One's faith is refined (purified) and strengthened. (b) Our faith in the power of God. (c) Rejoice in what God is doing in us (even though we experience "heaviness," that is, inward grief, the opposite word in meaning from "rejoice"). (d) The glorious appearance of Christ (the Rapture).

Section III—2. Joseph's thoughts seemed to focus on his relationship with God and with his master (how his sin would affect others); in this circumstance David apparently thought only of himself and of fulfilling his desires. Joseph considered the consequences of sin; David meditated on the pleasures of sin. Joseph had several opportunities to yield to sin but didn't; David had several opportunities to turn away from sin but didn't. David deliberately chose to carry out his plan to fulfill his lusts, step by step.

3. Peace and restoration can come only through acknowledgment of sin and confession to God. David did this in 2 Samuel 12. (*Discuss*: Even when God forgives our sins, He does not always remove the consequences. What consequences did David have to bear for his spiritual defeat?)

4. (a) Because it can accomplish a more widespread spiritual destruction, his delight! The sin of fathers or husbands can have a devastating, lifelong spiritual impact on children or wives. A pastor's fall into sin can debilitate his church and damage the cause of Christ. (b) By praying that they will resist the temptations of the evil one and be kept from him (John 17:15).

LESSON 10

Section II—1. *1 Timothy 1:18, 19*—A good soldier, like Timothy, must fight well, holding to the faith (not backsliding) and maintaining a good conscience. (*Discuss:* How can a believer have a clear conscience?) *1 Timothy 6:12–14*—Again, a steadfast soldier must be involved in the fight. (Don't abandon your post!) Like Christ, we are to remain faithful until the end of our mission, not backing down from our calling (Hebrews 12:2). *2 Timothy 4:7*—A dependable warrior, like Paul, will *finish the course* well.

2. *James 1:12*—When we endure trials and testing, we will be blessed with the crown of life. *1 Peter 4:1–7*—Christ, our Captain, has suffered as well; suffering hardships will purify us from sinful lusts of the flesh. *1 Peter 4:12–19*—As we are called to share in Christ's sufferings, we will also share in His glory.

3. He trusted in the name of the Lord and in God's power to deliver.

4. His true friend Jonathan came to him and "strengthened [David's] hand in God." Jonathan used his words to encourage, and he promised to stick by his friend. (*Discuss*: Why do believers withdraw from fellowship or avoid other Christians when discouraged?)

5. He encouraged himself in the Lord. (*Discuss*: What did he do in verses 7 and 8 that is an example to us?)

6. (a) "Swallow me up," "oppresseth me," "I am afraid," "my wanderings," "my tears." (b) "In God have I put my trust," "I will praise," "I will not be afraid," "I will praise his word."

7. (a) They were mocked and ridiculed for their efforts; they became the target of enemy opposition and attack. (b) They were determined to overcome; they had a *mind* (remember, that's where it starts!) to work; they labored and persevered. (c) They prayed and set an around-the-clock watch for enemy attack. (d) The people worked and defended themselves at the same time. They also made sure they could communicate and get help quickly in times of need. (e) Their power and deliverance would come from God. (*Discuss*: Notice that both God and the people were involved in the fight. How do Christians sometimes become passive about their part in a fight, but expect God to deliver them?) (f) God brought their schemes to nothing. (*Discuss*: Why do you think an actual attack never materialized? Can you make a spiritual parallel regarding this fact?)

8. *Galatians 5:24*—Because we are Christ's, we have the power to be "dead" toward the lusts of the flesh. (We overcome as we "abide in Christ.") *1 John 5:4*—Because of our new birth and our faith, we have already overcome the world. (We need to "abide" in our identity "in Christ" to continue to overcome!) *1 John 5:18*—Because we are begotten of God, the wicked one cannot touch us (unless *we allow* him to by our ignorance and apathy or *God allows* him to test our faith).

9. *Verse 31*—God is for us; He is on our side. *Verse 32*—He didn't hold back His only Son but gave Him over to death so we might receive all the blessings of God's mercy and grace, without reservation. *Verse 33*—No one can bring any charge of sin against us to separate us from God (as Satan, the accuser, seeks to do!). We are justified (declared "not guilty" of all our sins). *Verse 34*—Similarly, no one can condemn us if we sin now, because Christ is our intercessor (1 John 2:1, 2). *Verses 35–37*—No situation that this world or man or even nature can throw at us can separate us from our Lord's love. (Note: *Wycliffe Bible Commentary* states that the Greek words translated "we are more than conquerors" mean "we are in the process of winning," or "we are winning a most glorious victory.") (*Discuss*: According to verse 37, what is the only way we can achieve victory?) *Verses 38, 39*—Even when facing the forces of evil or the devastating effects of sin in life or physical death or any perceivable obstacle in the universe, *still* the love of Christ is able to reach us and preserve us!

10. *Revelation 2:7*—They will eat of the tree of life and live forever (Genesis 3:22). *Revelation 2:11*—They will not be hurt by the second death (Revelation 20:14). *Revelation*

2:17—They will be given "hidden manna" to eat and a white stone with a new name upon it. *Revelation 2:26–28*—They will rule with Christ. *Revelation 3:5*—They will be clothed in white and have their names confessed by Christ before the Father. *Revelation 3:12*—They will be "pillars" in God's temple (eternal place of worship) and will never leave His presence; they will bear His new name. *Revelation 3:21*—They will share in His throne.

Section III—2. Suggested answers: being available to listen or talk, praying, telling them you are praying, sending a note of encouragement. (*Discuss*: Why do some believers stop attending church during rough times? How can we help them?)

3. (*Discuss*: Why do we tend to draw away from the Lord at such times? How does this play into Satan's "game plan"?)

4. (a) We need to pray to seek God's enabling, guidance, and power to handle the situation. We cannot handle our difficulties in our own strength! We may also pray to be kept from the evil one. (b) Recall that 1 Peter 5:8 tells us to be vigilant, watchful. Satan attacks those who are ignorant, unprepared, and weak. If we think we are not vulnerable to Satan's schemes, we will fall prey. (c) They have to both work and pray side by side. All must do their part! They must pray for one another and cooperate with one another as they serve, appreciating the value of each "soldier-worker."